DOWN, DIRTY AND DIVINE

A SPIRITUAL RIDE THROUGH LONDON'S UNDERGROUND

REV. STEPHANIE CLARKE

To Beth & Benita
Blessings to your
sweet sisters in
sobriety on
Shine on
love
Rev.
Steph

Matador
9 Priory Business Park
Kibworth Beauchamp
Leicestershire LE8 0RX, UK
Tel: (+44) 116 279 2299
Fax: (+44) 116 279 2277
Email: books@troubador.co.uk
Web: www.troubador.co.uk/matador

ISBN 978 1780882 994

British Library Cataloguing in Publication Data.
A catalogue record for this book is available from the British Library.

Typeset in Adobe Garamond Pro by Troubador Publishing Ltd
Printed and bound in the UK by TJ International, Padstow, Cornwall

Matador is an imprint of Troubador Publishing Ltd

For the healing of the shadow in

Person

Place

and

Planet

Read what people are saying about

"DOWN, DIRTY AND DIVINE
A SPIRITUAL RIDE THROUGH LONDON'S UNDERGROUND"

"Rev. Stephanie Clarke has written an extraordinary book - one of profound wisdom and vision. Skillfully, she helps us to heal the wounds in our own hearts while shining the light of awareness on the dark shadow of underground London. Her gifts of writing, speaking, and teaching spiritual principles are expressed so graciously, touching every soul who comes into her presence. She is truly a blessing to the world!"
Savanna Riker, Religious Science Practitioner, Cairo, Egypt

"Rev. Stephanie Clarke radiates love and joy in her teaching, speaking, counselling and writing. This book is a must read that will open you to the blessings of her radiant consciousness."
Rev. Dr. Joan Steadman - Spiritual leader, Oakland, CA, USA

"Rev. Stephanie Clarke has always been a straight-ahead individual with her feet firmly planted in spiritual soil…her book is equally forthright and grounded in spiritual principle."
Rev. Hilde L. Brooks - Senior Pastor, Center for Spiritual Living, Antelope Valley, Lancaster, CA, USA

TESTIMONIALS

"Rev. Stephanie Clarke is a brilliant teacher, extraordinary minister and inspiring speaker. She is also delightful, charming and witty! But what I really wanted to talk about is how incredibly sexy she is, so full of "IT" and with a twinkle in her eye, and an appetite for life that this one lifetime cannot possibly satisfy..."
Rev. Nancy Zala, ordained New Thought minister at the Agape International Spiritual Center, and author of "The Joy of Affirmative Prayer," Los Angeles, CA, USA

Rev. Stephanie Clarke is an outstanding "Truth Teacher." Her life exemplifies the very highest regard for the Sacred and Holy all around us."
David Silverstein – Community Builder and Agape Licensed Spiritual Practitioner, Los Angeles, CA, USA

"Rev. Stephanie was one of my first teachers at Agape. Her warm and witty way of communicating ideas was easy for me to understand. I love and honor her for the truth that she lives and the inspiration she gives to others."
Brenda Lee Eager - singer/songwriter/actress/speaker, Los Angeles, CA, USA

"A true citizen of the world, demonstrating the Oneness of us all."
Rev. Bob Grabowski, San Diego, USA

Rev. Stephanie is amazing: a true world citizen and spiritual light who travels the globe bringing insight, wisdom and healing to all..."
Rev. Alice Bandy, The Heart of Teaching Center, Encinitas, CA, USA

"One counselling session with Rev. Stephanie literally changed my life..."
Melanie Hall - School Teacher & Librarian, Johannesburg, S. Africa

"'When the student is ready the teacher comes' is truly how my relationship started with the Reverend Stephanie..."
Philippa Sparrow – Alternative Health Therapist, Johannesburg, S. Africa

"I remember visiting her Science of the Mind gathering (Soul Home) in Johannesburg, South Africa...I felt I was at the beginning of something significant in my life. She created a space and set a standard... to build my present spiritual outlook."
Geoff Hall, IT Analyst, Johannesburg, S. Africa

"I know Stephanie to be a courageous student of life, bringing her zest and wisdom into all areas ...whether she is teaching a class or counseling a client or comforting a friend, she brings her whole self and is generously present and powerful."
Rev. Barbara Leger, Community Spiritual Leader, Temenos Science of Mind Center, Ukraine

DEDICATION

This book is dedicated to
my Dad
who knew London and loved her
both in her Dark and in her Light

******

CONTENTS

Foreword

I had a dream on September 25th, 2011. In the dream I was told to write a spiritual history of London using the Tube stations as my entry point. One week later, during my morning meditation, I was told that I should write a prayer at each Tube station site to heal the pain of the past. Furthermore, I was urged to publish the book before the 2012 Olympics in order to support the potential for transformation that such a large international convergence on London would afford.

As I got up from my meditation, I was reminded that Sir Christopher Wren, the grand architect of St. Paul's Cathedral, had envisioned London as the New Jerusalem and that this is, indeed, the awesome possibility that is waiting to unfold -- and can be realised with your conscious assistance.

I have tried to execute the instructions as best I could. I hope that you, the reader, find it interesting and inspiring. I also hope that it supports you on your own personal journey of transformation.

For me, the process of writing this book has been a spiritual homecoming to the city of my birth, and I am deeply grateful to you for your role in calling this book forth into manifestation.

Blessed be.

Rev. Stephanie Clarke
June 5, 2012

Prologue

This is a tale of one city. An extraordinary city with two lives: one above ground and one below, one light and one dark, one spiritual and one material. A city with a past. Goddess willing, a city with a noble future. This city is called London.

Many of London's greatest citizens, including Sir Isaac Newton, the scientist, and Sir Christopher Wren, who designed St. Paul's Cathedral, believed it was her destiny to be the New Jerusalem, a celestial city in a golden age, a place of harmony and love, prosperity and peace. They believed that it would be the place in which the lost tribes of Israel would gather again and that Jesus the Christ himself would choose London for his return to earth at the time of the Second Coming. Wren and his fellow freemasons in the Royal Society worked diligently towards this vision during the 17th and 18th centuries and the idea continued to be supported by British monarchs until World War II. But sadly, in the aftermath of war, in the bombed-out capital, buildings were rapidly thrown up without any awareness of sacred geometry or the grand spiritual purpose of the city. The vision of a New Jerusalem was buried underground, the flame almost extinguished.

Meanwhile, the shadow side of London, which, likewise, was *supposed to be* buried underground beneath the rich facade of majesty and landed wealth, was leaking through insidiously as race riots, anti-Semitism, religious hostilities, slavery, prostitution, murders, theft, overcrowded prisons, financial corruption, political rebellion, child abuse, broken homes, illiteracy, drug addiction, loneliness, unemployment and poverty in every permutation.

London and her citizens needed help. Her shadow of corruption and consumerism was killing her, draining her power. If she were going to rise to prominence, just like the brilliant phoenix from the grey ashes, and become a true City of Light, she would have to heal the darkness underground.

And how might she access that cavernous underworld from

her mighty teetering position of denial and forgetfulness?   Who would have thought that the triumph of engineering, during the glory days of the British Empire in the 19th century, would be the very access point she could exploit to confront and heal her shadow side: The London Underground.

The London Underground is almost 150 years old. It is 253 miles long and has penetrated its way through the complex layers of London's history, unwittingly opening up graves, tunneling through plague pits and disturbing the bones of generations past who had been laid there to rest.

Only they weren't resting...

They were stuck.

These lost generations were waiting for the Underground to be built so that they could rise up and finish telling their story to those who would listen – the underground builders, the workers, the commuters, the tourists, the travellers and you. They were waiting for the light – for those who could (and would) go into the nether regions to meet these souls in their own domain. They needed attention, compassion, understanding, and spiritual assistance to complete their journey and move mercifully to the next dimension.

And this is our work, yours and mine.

Later, there were those who met their end in the underground itself: the miners who bored the tunnels, the electricians, and the engineers who met their fate from loose earth, faulty wires, or imperfect machinery. The hungry gods of the underworld claimed their victims and punished the trespassers on their brooding temple sites.

Then, once the trains started running, there were even more "accidents" as some fell on to the tracks in front of oncoming trains. There were suicides: people hurtling themselves on to the tracks for relief from the pain they could not bear to hold. There were sexual assaults and murders on the trains themselves and on the dark, lonely platforms.

Finally, there were the disasters. During World War II, the Underground stations were used as air-raid shelters. Even though they were effective, so far below ground, they still could not withstand the force of a bomb's direct hit. Many breathed their last breath in those loud communal graves.

There are numerous strange tales of ghostly sightings, eerie feelings, foul smells, and plaintiff cries. Hardly surprising when you consider all the souls who have been buried in London's troubled past, but who have not been able to find peace until this moment.

This is a call for prayer, where you and I join in consciousness to acknowledge these beings and their unfinished stories ..... lifting them up from the dark tunnels of doom and endless wandering ...... offering them a helping hand .... and, with great love, ushering them forth into the tunnel of Light.

Schindler's Lift...

But wait, there is more.

Across these pages, like washing hung out to dry in the sunlight, are the stories of the humans who have made London's past both murky and magnificent. It is not "history." No, that would make it objective, something we could take a safe distance from and judge. Rather it is "our-story." All of it conveys the variations on a theme of self-preservation whether we were the victim or the oppressor, the prisoner or the jailer, the priest or the prostitute. Our secrets, our shame, our sullied selves, our fears, our phobias, our appalling behaviours and murderous motives – all this has been putrefying for eons and it will not be stuffed out of sight or out of heart.

Just as the stench used to rise from London's open sewers, so too the agony and the evil from that corrupted underworld leaks up and out through the streets of the City; it swirls around us, it swirls within us. We cannot get rid of it. It is our shadow. It will not rest. It is persistently there in all the forms we least enjoy. It is crying out for our attention and our compassion, to be seen and heard, accepted and embraced. It is crying out for prayer that it might be transformed into something lovely, something that could be loved - a prince instead of a toad...

"Transform or die" is the universal decree. And so in the year 2012 -- which was to be the end of the world according to the Mayan prophecy -- London hosted the World Olympic Games and, in accordance with her sacred destiny as a global city of Light, she called individuals and tribes from all corners of the planet to participate in these glorious celebrations of the ancient gods who dwelt upon Mount Olympus. With such a convergence of races and religions, cultures and nations upon London, under the guise of a grand, apolitical sporting event, it was clear that something of almighty proportions was destined to unfold.

That is why this book was written. That is why you have it in your hands now. You are a part of this unfolding.

How to Read this Book

This book is not normal!

Although plenty of books have been written about London, some dealing with her dark side and some with her light, nothing I have come across so far specifically attempts to heal and integrate the City's shadow at a spiritual level.

Furthermore, this book is a *spiritual* **tour guide** so, fortunately, you don't have to bring your body to London to visit the sites or do the inner healing work! The transformation takes place in your own mind so you can do the work from the comfort of your own consciousness - wherever you happen to be in the world.

In these pages you will find:

- a tour guide for spiritual explorers
- a London Underground travel guide
- a history book
- a prayer book
- a social commentary
- a metaphysical teaching tool
- a personal development workshop (my own included)
- an invitation to acknowledge and embrace the collective shadow at both the personal and planetary levels
- a journey of initiation
- a vision for a new future that we can co-create

It also has cool pictures!

No, I have never met a book like this before.

Precisely because this book is a little unusual, here are some guidelines for reading and working with the material in order to shower the greatest blessings upon yourself and the world.

Part 1 is your fore-tour. Part 2 is your journey to the depths.

Part I. The Fore-tour

Our multi-dimensional itinerary

We begin our spiritual ride through London by flying back through time to look at the religious origins of the Olympics and then we dive from the lighter side of our Greek ancestors into the dark mythology of the underworld and some painful religious concepts of death and hell.

We then sink deeper into the underworld of our own human nature – the shadow. From there we jet off to Jerusalem where the shadow side of human nature is on full bloody display in the centuries of conflict over possession of the holiest place on earth.

From the Holy Land, we take a brief trip to the Mayan culture of South America and their calendar, which is calculated to end in December 2012. The question upon us is: are we approaching the end of time or simply the end of time as we know it?

To expand our vision of what is possible, we then time-travel to the end of the New Testament and the Book of Revelations with its shining prophecy of the New Jerusalem, the celestial city of Light.

From this high and holy space, we float back to earth, to London, and to the inquiry of this book: could London be the New Jerusalem, the focal point of the Second Coming? We then explore together the various interpretations of the Second Coming from a religious and from a spiritual perspective.

From there, we leap on to the Underground and learn more about its 19th century origins, its developments and its disasters over the last 150 years as well as some of the spirits who are still wandering about its stations.

Since you and I are about the business of healing London's shadow, I take you into my "church on the page" and give you an overview of my spiritual approach to this work including an introduction to the power of affirmative prayer. Together, we will then drop down deep into the inner planes of consciousness and silently say a prayer for the healing of the London Underground.

Then I suggest some ways for you to open up as a beneficial presence for all whom you encounter while you are travelling on the Tube through London's underground world.

Next I introduce you to a new branch of the global travel industry, which I am conceptually launching in this book – SPIRITOURISM: an invitation to travel with the intention to give and to serve.

Finally, I put forward an outrageously heretical notion, according to the traditional religious viewpoints, but something critical for you to consider. Read on.

Part 2. The Journey to the Depths

Just as the Holy City of the New Jerusalem has 12 gates in the wall encircling the City, this book also has 12 gates: they are the Underground Stations that will take you on the journey into the realms of the Unknown and Unacknowledged, the Forgotten and the Unforgiven.

In the Catholic Faith, there are 12 Stations of the Cross. These are meditations on Jesus the Christ's path to his crucifixion, as he carried his cross, through the city of Jerusalem along the Via Dolorosa (the Way of Sorrows). Endeavouring to be non-denominational, I have called the 12 Tube stations in this book "the 12 Stations of the Cosmic Christ."

For the sake of ease, I have numbered each station but you don't have to follow them in any particular order – only as you are moved from within. However, if you go to St. Paul's Station, I do suggest going to the Old Bailey, Newgate and St. Sepulchre, in that order, followed by a trip to Marble Arch Station and the site of the Tyburn Hanging Tree. You might save the best till last and visit St. Paul's Cathedral at the end of your journey!

There is a chapter about each "city gate" – a Tube station that will lead you deep down into a part of London where your consciousness is desired and required to lift the pain of the ages. The site may be inside the actual Tube station itself or, in some cases, it might be a short walk away but, in every case, the site is underground, hidden from view, buried in history.

There will be directions for finding each site. Once you have read up on the relevant historical information, you will see a section called **"Reflection."** Here you will find some ideas and intuitions about the healing work that is upon us in this place.

Before we move into prayer, you will see a list of ways that the human sense of separation is showing up at this site e.g.

"Sense of separation (sin): greed, entrapment, powerlessness etc."

One of my teachers, now "on the other side of the Veil," Joel Goldsmith, said that the only sin we have to deal with is a sense of separation from God because all unloving thoughts, words and deeds arise from that.

Directly below that, you will find a list of the **"Spiritual Principles"** that we will focus on in the prayer to counteract and dissolve the appearances of separation. These principles are alternative names for God and, as such, they start with a capital letter.

The next section is a **"Prayer"** for the healing of the trauma connected to the site you are visiting. Please find a quiet place nearby where you can contemplate the words of the prayer and speak your own, where you can deeply listen and surrender into the Light anything within you or around you that is ready to be released.

May the prayers in this book be a conduit to take you deeper within yourself and may they be a catalyst for you to make a connection with your own indwelling spirit. All things are possible for us and for the world in this inner state of communion.

There is a space for your **"Notes"** after the prayer. You are welcome to record your experiences at each site and add your own prayers or intuitive thoughts in the space provided. You are also invited to go to the website or visit my Facebook page or tweet.

(All contact information is at the end of the book.)
    See you there!

"Never doubt that a small group of thoughtful, committed citizens can change the world. Indeed, it is the only thing that ever has."
Margaret Mead

Part I

The Fore-Tour

"Travellers, it is late.
Life's sun is going to set.
During these brief days that you have strength,
be quick and spare no effort of your wings."

Rumi

2012 Olympics in London

"There is no city like London. It is a wonderfully diverse and open city providing a home to hundreds of different nationalities around the world. I can't think of a better place than London to hold an event that unites the world."

Nelson Mandela

London is the only city in the world that has, so far, been chosen to host the Olympics three times! The first Olympic games in London were in 1908, the second in 1948. The opening ceremony for the third Olympics will be on July 27, 2012 and the closing ceremony on August 12.

It is interesting to look at the ancient origins of the games and to see how the religious myths about their origin tie in with the theme of London as the New Jerusalem heralding a golden age.

Religious Origins of the Olympics
There are many myths about the origins of the Olympics; the most prevalent is that the Greek gods themselves, in their sacred dwelling place atop Mount Olympus, initiated the games. Some historians believe that the Games started in the 8th century BCE at Olympia on the Peloponnesian peninsula in Greece.

Surprisingly, despite the traditional Greek celebration of male physical strength and prowess in the domain of athletics, the first Games, (according to Pausanias, a 2nd century CE Greek traveller) began as an annual foot race of young women competing to become the priestess in the temple dedicated to the goddess, Hera. The second race was started later in order to establish a male consort for the new priestess who would then participate in the sacred rituals at the temple.

The Olympics evolved into a series of athletic competitions in honour of the God Zeus. They were held every four years as they are today. In a time of constant warring between the Greek city-states, a political truce was called for the duration of the Games so that athletes were allowed to travel in safety from their homes to compete. Despite the fact that the games were supposed to be a celebration in honour of the gods, politics still came into play. Sound familiar?

There is one particular myth about the Games that concurs with the theme of the Messianic Age. The story goes that even though the Olympics were usually held every four years, they were discontinued for reasons unknown. The Oracle of Delphi announced that the people had strayed from the gods and this had caused plague and war. She instructed that the Games should be restored and this would end the plague and initiate a time of peace. The Games were resumed.

Sadly, by CE 435, in an attempt to impose Christianity as the State religion of Greece, either Emperor Theodosius, or his grandson Theodosius II, had stopped the Olympic Games.

The site of Olympia remained until an earthquake destroyed it in the 6th century CE.

The Nature of the Underworld

Let us now examine some of our fears, myths and cultural concepts associated with the Underworld.

The Underworld is a place of:

Death Regardless of religious beliefs or cultural traditions, people around the world bury their dead in the ground – both corpse and ashes. The body of flesh decomposes and becomes one with the earth while the spirit of the deceased flies free and becomes one with the cosmos.

Discarnate Spirits The place of death is also haunted by ghosts; souls who have not come to peace and not seen, or surrendered to, the tunnel of light that will lead them to the next dimension of unfolding. They cling to the earth, stuck between the worlds.

Disappearing All manner of people, including miners, explorers, hikers and archaeologists, are swallowed up by pitch black underground caverns while the compassionless rocks silence their cries for help.

Fear Not only because of its association with death, spirits and eternal wandering is the underworld a place of fear. The physical darkness, the heat, the lack of both fresh air and light make it a place where claustrophobia and the terror of suffocation and entrapment abound.

Mythology - Hades and Pluto In ancient Greek mythology, Hades is the god of the Underworld, the domain of death and darkness, secrets and shadows. The name Hades later came to mean "the abode of the dead" rather than the name of its ruler. All souls went to Hades, regardless of their good or bad deeds whilst alive.

Hades was also called "Plouton," meaning "Rich One," because the Underworld is the domain of precious metals and precious stones. The Romans Latinized this name as Pluto and associated Hades/Pluto with their own underworld gods and the abode of the dead.

The name "Pluto" has been given to the dwarf planet furthest from the sun because it is in permanent darkness.

Tartarus was the name of the ancient Greek god who ruled the dark abyss *below* the Underworld that was used as a dungeon of torment and suffering. In ca 380 BCE, in his Socratic dialogue called "Gorgias," Plato wrote that the souls were judged after death and those that received punishment were sent to Tartarus.

In Roman mythology, Tartarus is the place where sinners are sent. In his epic, "The Aeneid," the poet Virgil describes Tartarus as a gigantic place, surrounded by the flaming river Phlegethon and triple walls to prevent sinners from escaping from it.

Hell In many religious traditions, and also in popular culture, the Underworld is associated with hell, governed by the Dark Lord, Satan or the Devil, who is usually identified by his goat-like features: horns, cloven hooves and a tail.

The term "Hades" in Christian theology (and in New Testament Greek) is parallel to the Hebrew "Sheol" meaning "grave" or "dirt-pit", and refers to "the abode of the dead." The Christian concept of "hell," however, is more accurately described by the Greek concept of "Tartarus."

For Christians and Muslims, Hell is a place of endless suffering and punishment in the afterlife – the miserable result of evils committed whilst one was alive. The Jews, however, believe that Hell is a place where they will be judged but they can, at least, move on after a period of one year. (Big plus!)

Fire Hell is often associated with eternal fire. Is that
* because the ancients understood that the earth got hotter the

Fig. 1: Prophet Muhammad, along with Buraq and Gabriel, visit Hell, and see "shameless women" being eternally punished for exposing their hair to the sight of strangers. For this crime of inciting lust in men, the women are strung up by their hair. Persian, 15th century.

further one buried underground, and they concluded that there was an eternal fire in the depths of the earth?

- or because they witnessed "hellfire and brimstone" spewing from the mouth of erupting volcanoes and assumed that this fiery mass was everywhere under the surface of the earth?

- or because of the tradition in Jewish culture of burning rubbish outside the city walls of Jerusalem in the Valley of Hinnon, known as Gehenna, and dumping dead bodies here to be destroyed in the flames? These burning corpses once belonged to people who had died without hope of any salvation – the ones who had committed suicide.

Initiation In the great Mystery Schools of the Ancient World attached to the public temples of Eleusis in Greece, Thebes (now known as Luxor) in Egypt, and Ephesus in modern-day Turkey, the initiation journey often involved three days underground without light. The purpose was for the seeker to consciously face their worst fears and to experience their own death – the death of their humanhood, or the small self, before reemerging into the light, awakened.

The Dark Feminine There is a Sumerian initiation myth about the Queen of the Underworld, Ereshkigal, who is grief-stricken, angry, brooding, murderous, wild, dark, dirty and smelly. When her sister Inanna, Queen of Heaven, comes to visit, Ereshkigal has Inanna stripped, pecked to death and hung up on a meat hook to rot. To rescue their queen, Inanna's servants give Ereshkigal compassion for all her suffering in her dark, death-filled world. The compassion heals Ereshkigal's pain and she gives back her sister's corpse, which is then resurrected. Silvia Brunton Perera describes the myth in detail in her book "Descent to the Goddess: a Way of Initiation for Women," and recommends on page 8 that we make *"a descent into the spirit of the goddess, because so much of the power and passion of the feminine has been dormant in the underworld – in exile for five thousand years."*

Transformation Astrologically speaking, the influence of the planet Pluto on our individual and collective psyche brings about transformation through the death of ego. It destroys in order to renew. The shadow side of ourselves that we try to hide from others and ourselves by suppressing, denying and running from it, is brought into the light of Truth through our digging below the surface, driven by Pluto.

It is interesting that Pluto was discovered in 1930 at around the time when Sigmund Freud and Carl Gustav Jung were mining the realm of the deep sub-conscious through psychological exploration.

Regeneration The earth is the place where new life gestates during the winter months, where a seed is nurtured and sustained while it grows into a fully formed vegetable, fruit, herb, plant, tree or flower. From the perspective of Celtic mythology, Teresa Moorey writes on page 88 of "Paganism. A beginner's guide," "...the

Underworld is seen as a place of regeneration. In the Underworld was a cauldron of rebirth... The cauldron, of course, is a feminine symbol, but also has much to do with transformation, as ingredients are transformed into a brew."

Buried Treasure – Physical and Spiritual Apart from the fact that precious metals are located and mined below ground, many of us instinctively bury our treasure in the earth in the same way that we bury our dead. The ancient Egyptians buried their Pharaohs with all their earthly treasures to accompany them on the journey to their next incarnation.

From the psychological perspective, what if our "treasure" consisted of all the pains, fears, resentments, traumas, hurts, harms and disowned selves that we have buried in our deep subconscious as a mechanism for anaesthetizing ourselves against feelings we could not bear to feel?

Burying treasure is rarely meant to be a permanent strategy: treasure is usually buried with the intention of being accessed at a later date. Until we "dig up" our treasure by shining the light of pure awareness on our shadow self, that pain will drive us to react inappropriately to people and situations. We will project our pain "out there" and we will believe that we have to avoid/destroy/change those people, places and things in order not to feel more pain.

This book is an invitation to uncover the shadow-self. Thankfully we do not have to enter the dark space alone. All the readers of this book are in community, regardless of the date of reading. If we do pluck up the courage to enter our own underworld, protected in prayer, we will surely find our treasure: our own inner goldmine, our whole and sacred self. There is no greater wealth.

Our Personal
and Collective Shadow

Carl Gustav Jung, the Swiss psychologist, was the first to coin the term "shadow" to refer to those aspects of our unconscious mind that consist of repressed weaknesses, shortcomings and instincts. They represent the person we would rather not be, and so out of fear, ignorance or shame, we have denied their existence in ourselves.

In "Psychology and Religion," Jung wrote: "*Everyone carries a shadow and the less it is embodied in the individual's conscious life, the blacker and denser it is.*"

Some Jungians, such as Michael Fordham, maintain that "*The shadow contains, besides the personal shadow, the shadow of society ... fed by the neglected and repressed collective values.*"

The shadow is prone to projection; i.e., what we do not accept within ourselves is then projected out, on to others. The result? We accuse them of the very personality traits we cannot abide within our own nature.

According to Debbie Ford on page 6 of her book "The Dark Side of the Light Chasers," "*Jung believed that in order to become whole beings, 'we are obliged to struggle with evil, confront the shadow, to integrate the devil. There is no other choice.'*" Jung knew that such a journey required tremendous personal courage since we have to begin the descent with no guarantee of re-emergence into the light. However, he also knew from experience that every descent is followed by an ascent and a greater assimilation of the shadow, creating a more expansive whole human being.

In the same book, Ford takes the reader through a number of inner processes to heal the shadow. She recalls how a seminar leader said to her, when she was refusing to own the bitch in herself, "*What you don't own, owns you!*" On page 76, Ford writes, "*It takes compassion to own a part of yourself that you've previously disowned, ignored, hated, denied, or judged in others. It takes compassion to accept being human and having every aspect of humanity within you, good and bad. Ultimately, when you open your heart to yourself, you will find you have compassion for everything and everybody."*

Fig. 2:   *Yin Yang symbol is a visual depiction of the intertwined duality of all things in nature, a common theme in Taoism.*

The Holy City of Jerusalem

Temple Mount and the Rock

"Where there is much light, the shadows are deepest."
Johann Wolfgang von Goethe

"As the navel is set in the centre of the human body,
so is the land of Israel the navel of the world...
situated in the centre of the world,
and Jerusalem in the centre of the land of Israel,
and the sanctuary in the centre of Jerusalem,
and the holy place in the centre of the sanctuary,
and the ark in the centre of the holy place,
and the foundation stone before the holy place,
because from it the world was founded."
Midrash Tanchuma, Qedoshim

The Temple Mount in Jerusalem, also known as Mount Sion, is considered one of the holiest places on the planet for the three Abrahamic faiths of Judaism, Christianity and Islam. This large piece of elevated ground is believed to be a sacred portal to Heaven – the place where God can meet humanity and the place where the world began.

"...ye are come unto Mount Sion, and unto the city of the living God, the heavenly Jerusalem, and to an innumerable company of angels." Hebrews 12:22

In the Jewish and Islamic and Christian faith, the large rock of Temple Mount is thought to be the very site where Abraham had prepared to sacrifice his son Isaac (Hebrew) or Ishmael (Muslim).

"And he said, Take now thy son, thine only son Isaac, whom thou

Fig.3:   The Rock of Moriah, presumed to be The Foundation Stone, or a large part of it, taken inside the Dome of the Rock shrine.

lovest, and get thee into the land of Moriah; and offer him there for a burnt offering upon one of the mountains which I will tell thee of." Genesis 22:2

Abraham was stopped by God, commended for his faith and love, and told that blessings would flow forth to his descendants. The site has been known as Temple Mount ever since.

Temple Mount is also believed to be the place where God gathered earth to create Adam; where Cain, Abel and Noah offered sacrifices to God, where Jacob slept when he dreamed of angels going up and down the ladder.

"And he dreamed, and behold a ladder set up on the earth, and the top of it reached to heaven: and behold the angels of God ascending and descending on it." Genesis 28:12.

The Muslims believe that their prophet, Mohammed, left his footprint on this rock when, during his famous astral journey, he ascended to heaven from this sacred place to commune with Adam, Noah, Abraham, Moses, John and Jesus.

In 950 BCE, it was King David, father of Solomon, who made Jerusalem a holy city when he was instructed by God to build the first Jewish temple on Mount Moriah (Temple Mount), which would house the Ark of the Covenant.

"Then Solomon began to build the house of the LORD at Jerusalem in Mount Moriah, where the Lord appeared unto David his father, in the place that David had prepared..." 2 Chronicles 3:1.

The Ark is a wooden box, the container for the stone tablets with the Ten Commandments, which Moses had, purportedly, received from God on Mount Sinai. Jewish scholars believe that the Holy of Holies, the inner sanctum of the Jewish Temple in which the Ark was kept, would have been on the Rock.

Sir Isaac Newton (1642–1727), the noted English scientist, mathematician and theologian, was intrigued by the Jewish Temple's sacred geometry. He believed that King Solomon designed it under divine guidance and with insight that was beyond mere mortal capacity. In Isaac Newton's diagram (see Fig. 4) you can see the central space with the mark in the middle. It would have been the altar for the Ark – the Holy of Holies.

In 586 BCE King Nebuchadnezzar of the Chaldeans had the temple destroyed and forced the Jews to leave Jerusalem in captivity.

In 515 BCE, Cyrus, King of the Persians freed the Jews from bondage and allowed them to return to Jerusalem and rebuild the temple, which they did. In 70 CE the 2nd temple of Solomon was destroyed - this time by the Romans who had taken control of, and occupied, Jerusalem and the Holy Land.

The Western Wall is all that remains of the second temple and

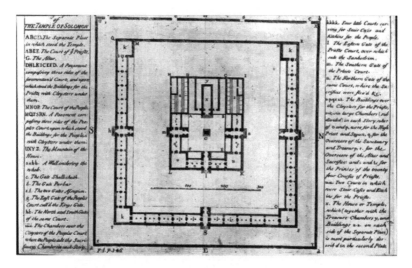

Fig. 4:   *Isaac Newton's diagram of Solomon's Temple, 1728*

it is more famously known today as "The Wailing Wall." It is the holiest site in the Jewish faith – the place where Jews go to pray, stuffing their prayer requests on scraps of paper into the cracks between those ancient stones.

Jewish texts record that the Mount will be the site of the Third Temple, which will be rebuilt with the coming of the Jewish Messiah.

In 312 CE, the Roman Emperor, Constantine the Great, converted to Christianity and ordered the construction of Christian churches throughout Jerusalem including the Church of the Holy Sepulchre, which is supposed to be on the site of Jesus' tomb. It was actually built over the site of the temple complex dedicated to Aphrodite, the Greek Goddess of Love, Beauty and Sexuality. (I wonder if the Christian pilgrims know that...?)

In 638 CE the Muslims took over the city and the caliph had a major Islamic shrine built – The Dome of the Rock - on the site of Solomon's Temple. This sacred site was considered to be the place of the Prophet Mohammed's ascension to Heaven. Its beautiful golden-domed roof, replicating the structure of the dome

Fig 5:   The Western Wall of Herod's Temple (aka Wailing Wall)

of the Church of the Holy Sepulchre, appears in all the classic cityscapes of Jerusalem.

The Muslims also re-built the Al Aqsa Mosque on the Temple Mount. This sanctuary had once been part of Herod's temple in 20 BCE.

Fig.6 :   The Dome of the Rock – Islamic Shrine

Fig. 7: The Dome of the Rock, Jerusalem, behind the Wailing Wall

When the Christian crusaders took the holy city of Jerusalem in 1099, their European leader, King Baldwin, converted the Al Aqsa mosque into his large palace and stables. The Knights Templar were invited to live there in 1118 and they stayed for most of the 12th century until 1187 while they carried out their secret excavations on the Temple Mount.

Currently, the Dome of the Rock and the Al Aqsa Mosque are under the control of the Muslims with the Rock being the most enviable piece of real estate.

Fig. 8: Roof terrace of the Church of the Holy Sepulchre

The Holy City of Jerusalem

17

The Palestinian – Israeli conflict for possession of the Holy City, and specifically the Temple Mount and the Rock, rages on to this day. Meanwhile the various Eastern Orthodox Christian denominations seem content to fight for dominance over the huge complex of the Church of the Holy Sepulchre.

If any of these religious groups could completely dominate the Holy City would it mean that they controlled the sacred access to God? Their religion would then be undeniably the most powerful – at least in their eyes. They would be right about God. How infinitely satisfying!

Many of us would prefer to be right and dead than happy and alive...

2012 Mayan Calendar

This is it!

We have arrived in the year 2012. The Mayan Prophecy is upon us. Will this be the end of the world, the end of the human race on the planet earth as we know it — beyond atomic bombs, floods and earthquakes, biological warfare, the contamination of our water sources? Are we in the cosmic days of the Apocalypse as predicted in the Bible?

The Mayans of South America were a very advanced people. As in every ancient culture, untrammelled by "civilisation," the capacity to tune into the spirit world and prophesy the future is normal and natural. The Mayans created both a Short Count and a Long Count Calendar. The Long Count calendar lasts 5126 years and it is due to end on 21 December, 2012. This doesn't necessarily mean that the world will end though.

When our western calendars run out on December 31 each year after 365 days, we confidently start a new cycle on January 1 without too much hype or craziness that the world is going to plummet into destruction – well depending on the intensity of one's hangover...

I like what Ian O'Neil had to say in "Universe Today," a website for news on space and astronomy:

"Archaeologists and mythologists ...believe that the Mayans predicted an age of enlightenment when 13.0.0.0.0 comes around; there isn't actually much evidence to suggest doomsday will strike. If anything, the Mayans predict a religious miracle, not anything sinister."

Personally, I believe we are at a choice point: we can choose to either grow spiritually, or continue destroying ourselves and our planet via greed and disregard for our fellow earthlings. We can choose to be conscious in our individual corners of the planet and responsible for what we are thinking, saying and doing or we can continue to recycle the same old conditioned patterns of behaviour. If we choose to wake up, then gradually clear drops of new thought, like spring water, will dilute the toxicity of both our inner and outer collective environment and, thereby, create a new world, one thought at a time.

The Apocalypse
and the New Jerusalem

The true definition of Apocalypse was a revelation to me. I had always understood it to mean "the disastrous and dramatic end of the world a la Hollywood," but here is the correct definition:

Apocalypse: *"a disclosure of something hidden from the majority of mankind in an era dominated by falsehood and misconception, i.e. the veil to be lifted."*

The word is derived from the Greek *apokalupsis*, a term applied to *"revelation or disclosure of what already exists, though hitherto it has been hidden, or only imperfectly known."*

"The Book of the Revelation of Saint John the Divine", the last book in the New Testament, is also known as the "Apocalypse of John". More commonly known simply as "Revelations," it is the place where John of Patmos describes his prophetic vision of the New Jerusalem. Is it a metaphor for Heaven or a state of cosmic consciousness or a vision of what is possible on earth?

The following Bible excerpt is Chapter 21:1-27 from the Book of Revelations (Lamsa Version).

1   *And then I saw a new heaven and a new earth; for the first heaven and the first earth had passed away; and the sea was no more.*

2   *And I saw the holy city, the new Jerusalem, coming down from God, prepared as a bride adorned for her husband.*

3   *And I heard a great voice from heaven saying, Behold, the tabernacle of God is with men, and he will dwell with them. They shall be his people, and the very God shall be with them and be their God.*

4   *And he shall wipe away all tears from their eyes; and there shall be no more death, neither sorrow nor mourning nor*

wailing, neither shall there be any more pain; for the former things have passed away."

5   *And he who sat upon the throne said, Behold, I make all things new. Then he said to me, Write; for these are the trustworthy and true words of God.*

6   *And he said to me, I am the Aleph and Tau, the beginning and the end. I will give freely of the fountain of living water to him who is thirsty.*

7   *He who overcomes shall inherit these things; and I will be his God and he will be my son.*

8   *But as for the fearful and the unbelieving and the sinful and the abominable and murderers and those who commit adultery and magicians and idolaters and all liars, their portion shall be in the lake that burns with fire and brimstone, which is the second death.*

9   *And there came to me one of the seven angels who had the seven bowls full of the seven last plagues, and he talked with me, saying, Come, I will show you the bride, the wife of the Lamb."*

10   *And he carried me away in the Spirit to a great and high mountain, and showed me that great city, the holy Jerusalem, descending out of heaven from God.*

11   *Having the glory of God, radiant as a brilliant light, resembling a very precious gem, like a jasper stone, clear as crystal.*

12   *It had a wall great and high and it had twelve gates, with names inscribed thereon, which are the names of the twelve tribes of the children of Israel.*

13   *On the east were three gates, on the north three gates, on the south three gates and on the west three gates.*

14   *And the wall of the city had twelve foundations, and on them were the twelve names of the twelve apostles of the Lamb.*

15   *And he who talked with me had a measuring rod of golden reed to measure the city and its gates and its wall.*

Fig. 9:   Golden Lamb of God seen on a gate in the Temple Church complex, London.
            (See also Fig. D in colour section)

16   And the city was laid foursquare, the length the same as the
         breadth; and he measured the city with the reed, twelve
         furlongs, twelve thousand paces. And the length and breadth
         and the height were equal.

17   And he measured the wall thereof, a hundred and forty four
         cubits, according to the measure of a man, that is, of the angel.

18   And the wall was constructed of jasper; and the city itself was
         pure gold, resembling clear glass.

19   And the foundations of the city walls were adorned with all
         kinds of precious stones. The first foundation was jasper, the
         second sapphire, the third chalcedony, the fourth emerald,

20   The fifth sardonyx, the sixth sardius, the seventh chrysolyte,
         the eighth beryl, the ninth topaz, the tenth chrysoprasus, the
         eleventh jacinth, and the twelfth amethyst.

21   And the twelve gates were adorned with twelve pearls, one for
         each of the gates, and each gate was made of a single pearl;
         and the great street of the city was of pure gold, as if it were
         transparent glass.

22   *But I saw no temple therein, for the Lord God Almighty and the Lamb are the temple of it.*

23   *The city has no need of the sun neither of the moon to shine in it, for the glory of God brightens it, and the Lamb is the lamp of it.*

24   *And the people who have been saved shall walk by that very light; and the kings of the earth shall bring their own glory and the honour of the peoples into it.*

25   *And the gates of it shall not be barred by day, for there is no night there.*

26   *And they shall bring the glory and the honour of the peoples into it.*

27   *And there shall not enter into it anything which defiles nor he who works abominations and lies; only those shall enter whose names are written in the Lamb's book of life."*

Down, Dirty and Divine

"Jerusalem"

by William Blake

"And did those feet in ancient time" is a short poem by the mystical poet, William Blake *(1757-1827)* from the preface to his epic "Milton: a Poem," one of his prophetic books. It was first printed in ca 1808. The poem was set to music in 1916 and is now famous as the anthem, "Jerusalem."

In the poem, Blake alludes to the popular legend that Jesus the Christ visited Glastonbury in Somerset with his uncle, Joseph of Arimathea, during the "lost years" i.e. the years between 12 and 30 when there are no records of him in the Bible. Blake, a Londoner like Sir Christopher Wren, was also a proponent of the idea that the Second Coming of Jesus the Christ would be in England where He would establish the New Jerusalem.

And did those feet in ancient time
Walk upon England's mountains green?
And was the holy Lamb of God
On England's pleasant pastures seen?

And did the Countenance Divine
Shine forth upon our clouded hills?
And was Jerusalem builded here
Among these dark Satanic Mills?

Bring me my bow of burning gold!
Bring me my arrows of desire!
Bring me my spear! O clouds, unfold!
Bring me my chariot of fire!

I will not cease from mental fight,
Nor shall my sword sleep in my hand,
Till we have built Jerusalem
In England's green and pleasant land.

Fig. 10: Folio 55r of the Bamberg Apocalypse depicts the angel showing John the New Jerusalem, with the Lamb of God at its centre. (See also Fig C. in colour section)

Down, Dirty and Divine

Could London be the New Jerusalem?

"Ye are the light of the world. A city that is set on a hill cannot be hid."

Matthew 5:14

Starting in the 6th century CE, there was a belief in England that London would be the New Jerusalem and I believe it is now time to resurrect this idea. I don't mean the old notion of a reincarnated physical Jesus alighting down on the Dome of St. Paul's, flanked by cherubs, smiling his approval of the new temple. I don't mean a Jesus who would teach scripture and then lead the masses of Londoners, (Brits plus all other nations and religions that are represented in London), into a mystical state whereby they could

✓ all get along,
✓ appreciate the unity in their diversity,
✓ have compassion and forgiveness for the ignorant attitudes of one another,
✓ make amends for harms done in the past for the last few thousand years which still dominate today,
✓ spontaneously form a beloved inter-faith community and
✓ generally live a joyous creative expanded life full of love, purpose, meaning and service.

But what if:

• the celestial city is not located in Jerusalem but in London?
• "celestial" does not mean somewhere in the sky beyond death – a Utopia that can never be reached except in the imagination, but a harmonious possibility that we can co-create?

- the celestial city could arise out of the reconciliation of all cultures, religions, nationalities, political persuasions and sexual orientations?
- you and I were to establish the celestial city within our own beings through the reconciliation between the light and the dark within us, between our public persona and our shadow?
- the masculine, mental sky god in all of us dared to enter the wound in the earth, in the dark depths of the feminine emotional body, the belly of the Mother Goddess, and offer Her presence and compassion for 5000 years of rage and suffering?
- the masculine and feminine polarities within us were re-united in love and worship?

London is the place where this transformational shift in consciousness could unfold, indeed, where it is unfolding even now: a shift in the personal, metropolitan, national and global awareness of Oneness.

"The Second Coming"

by Yeats

The following poem was written by William Butler Yeats (1865 – 1939) in the year 1919 in the aftermath of World War I.

The "beast" is more of a sinister prediction of the dark times of the Battle of Armageddon and the Anti-Christ, which precede the Second Coming of the Christ, according to the Bible.

TURNING and turning in the widening gyre
The falcon cannot hear the falconer;
Things fall apart; the centre cannot hold;
Mere anarchy is loosed upon the world,
The blood-dimmed tide is loosed, and everywhere
The ceremony of innocence is drowned;
The best lack all conviction, while the worst
Are full of passionate intensity.

Surely some revelation is at hand;
Surely the Second Coming is at hand.
The Second Coming! Hardly are those words out
When a vast image out of Spiritus Mundi
Troubles my sight: somewhere in sands of the desert
A shape with lion body and the head of a man,
A gaze blank and pitiless as the sun,
Is moving its slow thighs, while all about it
Reel shadows of the indignant desert birds.
The darkness drops again; but now I know
That twenty centuries of stony sleep
Were vexed to nightmare by a rocking cradle,
And what rough beast, its hour come round at last,
Slouches towards Bethlehem to be born?

The Second Coming

according to the three Abrahamic religions

"The truth was a mirror in the hands of God. It fell, and broke into pieces. Everybody took a piece of it, and they looked at it and thought they had the truth."

Rumi

The Jewish Perspective

The term Messiah means "anointed," referring to the anointing with holy oil of kings and priests in the Jewish tradition to symbolise their divine appointment. Later, it came to take on a more prophetic meaning: a leader anointed by God, a future king of Israel, descended from the royal lineage of David, who would rule the united tribes of Israel and usher in the golden age of global peace.

According to Jews, Jesus could not be the Messiah because he did not serve as a military leader who freed the Jews from the Roman occupation. Moreover, he died on the cross at the hands of the Romans, which would never have happened if he were the real Messiah. So according to the Jews, the Messiah is yet to come!

The Islamic Perspective

Jon R. Stone, quoting from the "Sahih Muslim" 41:7023 and the "Sahih Al Bukhari" 3:43:656 in his book "Expecting Armageddon: Essential Readings in Failed Prophecy" writes that Muslims believe Isa (Jesus) will return at a time close to the end of the world. He will descend in the midst of holy wars being fought by the Mahdi (literally "the rightly guided one"), against the al-Masîh ad-Dajjâl ("false messiah") and his followers. The place of Isa's descent will be east of Damascus. He will be dressed in yellow robes and his head will be anointed. Isa will join the Mahdi and will slay the Dajjal. Then everyone from the "People of the Book" (i.e. Jews and Christians) will believe in him. Thus, there will be one community comprised of all the Abrahamic faiths – a community of Islam. After the death of the Mahdi, Isa will assume leadership and will herald an age of universal peace and justice.

The Christian Perspective

According to Christians, Jesus is the Messiah, the Saviour, who will return to save his people (not only Jews) from sin and death. This interpretation of Messiah has nothing to do with the military prowess that the Jews and the Muslims associate with a Messiah. Jesus never claimed to be a military leader. In fact, he stood for the opposite: inner personal freedom through connection with the Source as opposed to outer political freedom gained through destroying enemies.

The unifying point is that all three religions hope that a divine leader from their ranks will show up and establish a reign of peace, whether by conquering the enemies on the outer level or the inner level.

The Esoteric Perspective

Rosicrucian Esoteric Christian teaching is the most relevant for me, partly because it speaks to my own metaphysical understanding and, partly, because Christopher Wren seems to have followed the Rosicrucian teachings as his spiritual path.

In the esoteric teaching, a distinction is drawn between "Jesus the man" and "Jesus the Christ" – the Christ being the true divine nature of all beings.

The Christ Within, therefore, is the true Saviour who needs to be born within every individual in order for humanity to evolve toward the *"new heavens and a new earth."* According to the Rosicrucians, the Second Coming is not in a physical body of a male figure looking like a human Jesus, but in the new *soul body* of each individual. This is to unfold during the Age of Aquarius –

a 2000-year period, characterised by Love and Wisdom, which began around the time of the new millennium.

Interestingly, the Theosophist, Alice Bailey, prophesied in 1946 that the Christ would return "sometime after CE 2025."

Fig.11 : Icon of the Second Coming.
          Christ is enthroned in the centre surrounded by the angels and saints, Paradise is
          at the bottom, with the Bosom of Abraham (left) and the Good Thief (right)
          holding his cross. (See also Fig. B in colour section).

The "Cosmic Christ" and the London Underground

"Everything that is in the heavens, on the earth, and under the earth, is penetrated with connectedness, penetrated with relatedness."

Hildegard of Bingen

Matthew Fox, the former Catholic priest who was excommunicated for his radical views that were contrary to the dogma of the Church, wrote a book called "The Coming of the Cosmic Christ." He speaks of this "coming" as a new dimension of consciousness being embodied by those who are developed and developing on their own personal and collective spiritual journey. He calls it *"the pattern that connects."*

Perhaps the London Underground is a perfect symbolic representation of this pattern that connects?

✓ It is not visible in the light but ever present beyond our surface awareness.

✓ It invisibly connects people, places and things throughout the metropolis.

✓ It is a network – all points are connected to all other points. Therefore, a blockage at one point affects the whole negatively. Similarly, an opening at another point affects the whole positively.

✓ The visible entry points are the stations above ground – like human beings who seem separate on the surface but all hark back to a shared consciousness.

✓ It consists of all colours of the rainbow, combining harmoniously together.

A Short History of the Tube

In the 1830s, Charles Pearson, a solicitor to the City of London and the MP for Lambeth, was the first to suggest a system of underground railways to relieve the congestion on the roads in London. Commuters travelling to London got off the over-ground steam trains at Paddington, Euston and King's Cross (the northern and western outskirts of the city), but there was no fast way for them to get into the city or across it.

Pearson's proposal was met with ridicule and resistance. According to Peter Ackroyd in his book "London Under" a popular preacher at the time predicted that "the forthcoming end of the world would be hastened by the construction of underground railways burrowing into the infernal regions and thereby disturbing the devil."

Nevertheless, 30 years later and, sadly, a few weeks after Charles Pearson's death, the Metropolitan Underground Railway was unveiled. It ran from Paddington to Farringdon and was the first underground system to be built in the world. The name Metro would become the name for all the other underground train systems that were subsequently constructed in the major cities across the planet.

The Underground's success initiated a frenzy of private companies building new lines under London. Inhabitants of the inner city slums on the path of the new lines were simply thrown out without compensation or re-housing. It was not until the London County Council was established in 1889 to manage the streets, transportation and public housing that these problems began to be addressed.

In 1890 the Stockwell Line ran the first trains powered by electricity. This meant that underground travellers no longer had to risk death from suffocation in the stench and the smoke of the underground steam trains.

In 1884 the Circle Line opened.

In 1900 the Central Line was inaugurated. It was nicknamed the "Twopenny Tube" for its flat fare and cylindrical tunnels. The "Tube" nickname was eventually transferred to the Underground system as a whole.

In 1911 the first escalator was opened at Earl's Court. It was the first moving staircase in London built to unite the platforms of the Piccadilly and District Lines. Travellers were terrified of using it, particularly getting off the escalator at the bottom.

In 1960 the Victoria Line was built connecting all the other lines in central London.

Today, the London Underground's eleven lines are divided into two classes:

1. The subsurface routes: The Circle, District, Hammersmith & City lines.
2. The deep-tube routes: The Bakerloo, Central, Jubilee, Northern, Piccadilly, Victoria and Waterloo & City lines.

Mass Deaths and Disasters on the Tube

In wartime (1939-1945)

Despite the fact that the Underground was not designed to be an air-raid shelter, it successfully protected thousands of Londoners during World War II - except in some unfortunate cases mentioned below:

Marble Arch On 16 September 1940, 20 people were killed by a bomb.

Balham On 14 October 1940, a bomb penetrated the road and tunnel at this Tube station, blew up the water mains and sewage pipes and killed 68 people.

Bank In 1941 a bomb dropped into the crypt at St. Mary Woolnoth, which is actually the ticketing hall of Bank Tube Station. The bomb bounced down the escalator and exploded on the platform killing 117 people.

Bethnal Green After an air-raid siren sounded in 1943, 173 people lost their lives when they began entering the tube station via the stairwell. Some missile testing was going on close by and, because the sounds were so close and unfamiliar, panic set in. People started rushing into the stairwell and when one woman near the bottom tripped and fell, the others behind her simply fell on top of her. In the blackout, and with inadequate lighting below ground and no handrail, the people at the top continued to rush in, crushing the ones below with their bodyweight.

Down, Dirty and Divine

In "peace" time 1945 -

Moorgate The Tube disaster occurred on 28 February, 1975, when the train driver drove at full speed past the station platform and directly into a brick wall at the end of the tunnel; 43 people were killed at the scene, either from the impact or from suffocation.

King's Cross On 18th November, 1987, 31 people were trapped and killed in a fire that started on a wooden escalator on the Underground but then erupted in the ticketing hall at street level. The cause of the fire is not known. It is believed that it started accidentally from a discarded match, even though smoking had already been banned.

Ghosts on the Tube

The Tube seems to be the place where ghosts spend their time and where they go to be seen, whether or not they originally met their end there...

Elephant and Castle (end of Bakerloo Line) There are two tunnels at the south end of the London Depot on the Bakerloo Line. One goes to Elephant and Castle and the other is a dead end. A plague pit is located behind that wall. No ghosts of plague victims have been seen but no workers are ever willing to go down there at night either. One underground employee did see a ghost at the Elephant and Castle terminus: a woman walked past him onto the train, but then disappeared although she could not have left the carriage without him noticing. Apparently, many of the Underground staff reported seeing her.

Aldwych This station was closed in 1994 because it was too expensive to refurbish the lifts. It used to be on the site of the Royal Strand theatre. Many people have seen the ghost who haunts the tracks at night. She is believed to be an actress.

Bank The "Black Nun" haunts this station. She is searching for her brother, Phillip Whitehead, who was a cashier at the bank and was executed in 1811 for forgery. It is suspected that this station is also built on a plague pit and this might explain why many workers and travellers report foul unexplained smells and feelings of sadness, concern and hopelessness.

Covent Garden Since the 1950s, many have seen the ghost of the actor, William Terris, who was stabbed to death near the Adelphi Theatre in the Strand, December, 1897. He is described as a tall man in a frock coat, tall hat and gloves, pacing the tunnels. It is said that he regularly visited a baker's shop that is on the site of the current Tube station.

Farringdon In 1758, a 13-year-old trainee hat maker, Anne Naylor was murdered by her trainer and the trainer's daughter. She has been nicknamed "The Screaming Spectre," because people still hear her cries echoing through the station.

Aldgate East This station is also on the site of a plague pit. An electrician made a slip and gave himself a massive electric shock. It knocked him unconscious. Apart from bruising his forehead, he was amazingly unharmed. His colleagues noticed that there was a half transparent figure of an old woman stroking his hair.

Vauxhall While the Victoria Line was being built at Vauxhall Station in 1968, a male figure, about 7 feet tall and wearing brown overalls and a cloth cap was regularly sighted. No one was able to identify him and he never let any of the workers get too close!

***

Time to Pray?

Now that all of these souls have begun to emerge on to the pages of this book and have your attention, it is time to address the subject of prayer so that we can offer them healing and release – if they choose it. In the next section, I will tell you a little about "Affirmative Prayer" and then I will share with you how you can be about your sacred work when you are travelling on the Tube or visiting the sites in the City of London, using this book as a guide.

The Power of Prayer

"When we begin to perceive the nature of God, we will know how to pray. When we know how to pray, all of God's grace will manifest Itself in our life because prayer is the connecting link between man and God. It is through prayer that we bring God's grace into our individual experience and are enabled to share it with others so that they, too, benefit in some degree by the Grace that we have received."

Joel Goldsmith

The salient message of the New Thought/Ancient Wisdom teachings, to which Science of Mind belongs, is the notion that "thought creates experience." And probably the most powerful gift of the Science of Mind teaching, compiled and articulated by Ernest Holmes from all the great world philosophies and religions, is **Spiritual Mind Treatment.** This is the Science of Mind term for "affirmative prayer."

In this approach to prayer, we do not beg or beseech a power outside ourselves to change our circumstances or the circumstances of our loved ones. Instead, we access the Power inside ourselves and affirm the Truth about the Divine Reality.

The Divine Reality is an eternal state of Being that is not affected by changing circumstances and conditions. So, for example, in the midst of appearances of poverty, Abundance Is. In the midst of appearances of death, only Eternal Life Is. In the midst of appearances of conflict, only Love Is.

The skill we have to develop is turning away from appearances and inwardly beholding the Divine Reality until it manifests itself in our earthly experience, which it eventually must. Truth will always outweigh the lies of shortage, death and conflict and, as the Master Teacher, Jesus the Christ, reminded us:

"*...as thou hast believed, so be it done unto thee.*" Matthew 8:13.

In a Spiritual Mind Treatment or an affirmative prayer, there are 5 distinct steps:

1. **Recognition** of One Power

2. **Unification** of myself with the One Power and with whomever I am praying for

3. **Realization** and affirmation of the Divine Reality which is behind all appearances to the contrary

4. **Thanksgiving** that the purpose of my prayer is already accomplished

5. **Release** of my prayer into the Law of Mind - in faith that the answer is already manifesting on the physical plane of our human experience.

You will notice that when I speak or write my prayers, I speak from "I" – the voice of Divine Truth within me - as much as I can embody and articulate at the time of writing. When you read the prayers, I suggest that you also read from the "I" place within yourself.

Since there is only One Mind, you and I do not have to be together physically. We simply have to be gathered in intent. Even now, you and I are joined in consciousness to know the Truth and to be a blessing and an instrument of forgiveness and compassion for ourselves and the world. I believe this is what the master, Jesus the Christ, meant when he said: *"For where two or three are gathered together in my name, there am I in the midst of them."* Matthew 18:20.

Thank you for being willing to gather with me and birth a new possibility in our midst.

Please join with me in prayer now.

An Affirmative Prayer
for the Tube

There is One Power and One Presence. Life Divine and Whole, Present everywhere and Perfect at every point within Itself. It is the Alpha and the Omega without beginning and without end. It has never been born therefore It can never die. It is Immortal Infinite Life.

I AM a perfect emanation of that Divine Presence that governs the Universe. I can never be separate from It nor can It ever be separate from me. It is the Power that lives Its Life as me. I AM Immortal, in Truth, and so is every sacred soul who has ever appeared or will ever appear on the planet.

Knowing that I am one with the Infinite Presence and also one with every person who ever reads this prayer and one with everyone who ever travels or works on the London Underground (past, present or future), I now speak this Word for all beings who have made their transition on the Underground or been buried in or around the Tube network. I declare for all these souls that all appearances of physical, emotional or mental trauma surrounding their transition, are now dissolved in the light of pure awareness. I behold them all as immortal spirits, free of the chains of humanhood, complete with their incarnation on earth and moving forward on their spiritual journey with Grace and ease.

For the disembodied spirits who are still seemingly travelling on the Tube, I know that they are now embraced by the Divine Light at the end of the tunnel leading from the realm of earth to the realm of Infinite Reality. I declare for them all "Peace, be still!" and know that their wanderings are now over. This Word of prayer is the healing balm that bathes their souls in Peace.

I speak this Word also for the Tube network itself, for the stations, the trains, the tunnels, the tracks, the platforms, the lights, the escalators, the ticket machines, the lifts, the hidden

Down, Dirty and Divine

machinery and computerised networks that drive the trains each day. I declare that the very nature of this Tube system is Perfect Function. There are no delays, accidents or disasters in Spirit, there is only perfect flow. I know that the entire Tube network of stations and tunnels, trains and travellers is held in the very palm of the Divine Hand and no harm can come nigh.

Furthermore, I declare that every journey taken on the Tube is in essence a spiritual journey. Therefore, I speak this Word for the Tube as a container for the awakening of all travellers and workers. It is the underground of being, the deep and vital core of transformation in consciousness. I declare that this Word acts as a laser beam of light, dissolving any and all appearances of death, negativity, pain, burden or sorrow from the mental atmosphere of the Underground. All is healed. All is well.

I give thanks now for the healing and release of all souls who have ever transitioned or been buried in or around the Tube network. I give thanks for the Light being shown to all beings who were previously stuck between the worlds.

I give thanks for the Perfect Function of the Tube, carrying all souls safely to their destination of spiritual realization, to the place where they are alive awake and aware and where they can be of maximum service, fulfilling their destiny on earth, as it is already done in Heaven.

Having spoken this Word in faith, believing, I now release It to the outworking of the Universal Law and know that It cannot return to me void but must return fulfilled. And so It is and so I let It be. Amen.

Travelling on the Tube – Consciously

"And you?
When will you begin that long journey into yourself?"

Rumi

As you move through the ticket machines with your travel card or Oyster card, remind yourself that you are now entering the inner realms of consciousness. You have paid a few pounds to be carried through the Underground of London – an engineering feat that cost thousands of pounds and many lives to bring about.

As the escalator takes you down into the London underbelly, consciously soften your own underbelly in a state of surrender. Allow yourself to open to the dark side of the city. Remember that you are moving through many dimensions of time and experience.

Ask
- to be reminded of the 23rd psalm: *"Yea, though I walk through the valley of the shadow of death, I shall fear no evil for Thou art with me."* Yes, the I AM of your being is with you, has brought you here to do this sacred work. It has gone ahead of you to prepare the way and is even now revealing to you exactly what you need to know,
- to be guided as you enter the infinite depths of the earth and your own being so that the journey brings you whatever you need to see, hear, understand and release,
- to be healed in the depths of your being,
- for all beings whom you encounter to be healed (knowing that not all beings are visible to you in the physical),

- for your connection with the consciousness of London to be healed. That includes not only this incarnation but any previous incarnations and
- to be an instrument of prayer.

Whatever you choose to do, remember that you are here to be a beneficial presence by perceiving all your fellow Tube travellers as sons or daughters of the Most High.

- Bless everyone you meet as a brother or a sister in spirit
- Bless the underground workers, past present and future
- Bless the building and those who constructed it and are now maintaining it for your safety
- Bless the CCTV cameras and those who watch the hours of film, and
- Bless the ticket barriers and the escalators – they give you access to and from the shadow world.

While you are on the escalator
- Bless those who are ahead of you and bless your future
- Bless those who are behind you and bless your past and
- Bless those who cross your path on the escalator going in the opposite direction, especially those whose eyes you meet
- Bless everyone who had any part in creating the Tube and transforming to make it safe, light and comfortable so that you could take this journey today. Everything has been done on your behalf. It was all in place, waiting for you to enter in – on this day and at this very hour.

"Mind The Gap"

When you get on and off the Tube and hear the words "Mind the Gap," even though it is that famous warning to be aware of the gap between the train and the platform, I invite you to reinterpret

Fig. 12: *"Mind the Gap" written on the edge of the platform to prevent travellers from falling down on to the tracks as they step on to the train. (See also Fig. H in colour section.)*

it as a spiritual message to you from your Indwelling Spirit.

Your mind is your instrument of awareness. The "gap" is the sense of separation or sin that is ever ready to tempt you and me into believing that we are alone and powerless, victims of forces beyond our control.

So the full alternative instruction would be: "Pay attention to the ever-present temptation to fall into a sense of separation."

I prefer "Mind the Gap."

Divine Shorthand?

"Alight Here!"

Another piece of Divine Shorthand on the Underground is the phrase "Alight here." Before the Tube train pulls into a station, especially in central London, a recorded message tells you to "Alight here for …," then the voice tells you the Tube lines you can connect to and which important buildings, such as museums, are close by above ground.

My first thought about that announcement was very judgmental: Why can't she just say "Get off the train here for…" instead of using that hoighty-toighty language that no foreigner would understand unless they had studied Shakespeare? Then I saw the role of the Divine behind this antiquated use of language. It is the instruction to "*Be* a light here." So, as we get off the train, we are consciously aware that we are "being a light" in that area of the Underground and above ground too.

Spiritourism:
a new way to travel

"But rather seek ye the Kingdom of God and all these things shall be added unto you."

Luke 12:31

As I mentioned earlier, this book is my conceptual launching pad for a new branch of the global travel industry: SPIRITOURISM. The meaning is simply: *"travelling to give."*

If you were a regular tourist, you would be coming to London to consume – to take in the sights, to shop, to eat, to soak up the culture. You would want to enjoy the theatrical productions, to stimulate yourself, to add to your rich bank of cultural and historical knowledge, to be entertained and to be served. You might be coming to escape your everyday life, your family, your boss and / or your neighbours. You might be coming to have fun, let your hair down, be mad and uncontrolled for a while because you are not on your home territory with people who know you and judge you and monitor your social behaviour. You paid your money and you are buying an experience of aliveness, joy, connection, inspiration, satisfaction, relaxation etc. Only all of it is empty in the end.

You might be coming to London on a pilgrimage to experience the great holy sites of St. Paul's Cathedral, Westminster Abbey, St. Bartholomew's Priory. If this is the case, you would still be coming to consume and to get something – only that something would be a little more intangible than a regular tourist's desires: renewal, enlightenment, upliftment, spiritual regeneration and refreshment. You would want something to take back with you that would enrich your inner and outer life.

Spiritourism, or *"travelling to give,"* means that you come with the opposite intention from regular tourism or even a pilgrimage. You come to give and not to get. You start your journey with a prayerful intention to be of service and to be a beneficial presence wherever you are and whomever you are with, beholding the divinity in all people, places and things along the way.

The spiritual irony of this idea is that, in the act of giving, you receive all the joy, satisfaction, upliftment, inspiration, connection etc. that regular tourists are looking for and cannot get by trying to consume something outside of themselves.

Even if you only picked up this book after you arrived in London and did not knowingly come here to give of yourself, consider the possibility that you are here to consciously cleanse past wounds, unearth buried memories, hear the cries of the persecuted and the lost (in your own soul and in the soul of the city) and then to pray for it all. You can transform the essential purpose of your journey at any moment you choose.

"When you do things from your soul, you feel a river moving in you, a joy."

Rumi

Your Divine Appointment

"When an idea reaches critical mass, there is no stopping the shift its presence will induce."

Marianne Williamson

There are no accidents.

This book has come into your hands by right of consciousness. It was written with you in Mind. It was written for you to assist in the healing of self, the City of London and the planet.

Please consider that whatever the pretext was that got you here – to this book and / or to London itself, that you have been moved by a Higher Hand in order to play your part in this Divine Commission of global transformation. Perhaps you came for the Olympics? Maybe it was a business trip? A visit to friends or family? A sight-seeing holiday? A culture fest of art, music, museums and theatre? Spirit will use whatever excuse It has to in order to fool you and bring you to where you need to be for your greatest good and the greatest good of the Whole.

Perhaps your very presence in London (physical or spiritual) had been mandated *before you were even born* because you were the one who had chosen to be chosen to be a part of this grand healing journey?

Even if you are reading this page many miles from the misty isle of the ancient Celts, with no conscious intention to visit London, nevertheless your willingness to align yourself with the prayers in this book forms a critical piece of the healing work that is being called forth.

There is no time or space in the Divine Mind. As Ernest Holmes tells us on page 94 of the Science of Mind textbook, *"...whatever is known at one point in It (Mind) is known at all points instantly!*" You don't have to be in the physical location of London to know the Truth. You just have to pray.

What can you conceive of as a possibility for London? And for yourself? Everything within you will organise itself around that expanded vision of possibility. It is part of our Divine make-up that we can think outside our circumstances. Now, thinking *beyond* present circumstances, plants new seeds in the fertile soil of the Universal Mind, generating new tomorrows. The past is not the precedent. The future can unfold in any direction that we determine. As the Master, Jesus the Christ, said: *"And I, if I be lifted up from the earth, will draw all men unto me."* John 12:32.

What if you and I are the midwives of the Second Coming? By that I mean "the revelation of the Christ Consciousness of Love and Unity in 51% of the global population."

What if you, yourself, are a messiah - one who has been appointed to shift the global consciousness to 51% positive through your next loving thought, your next compassionate response, your next generous gift, your next honest admission, your next shining act of courage or your next burst of joy?

Let's assume we are all embryonic messiahs, all whole and holy, all anointed by the Source to fulfil our own sacred appointments on earth, all developing and awakening to our true potential as gods and goddesses, sons and daughters of that Infinite Creative Power.

We should begin our mission with London, knowing that the focus of our attention here will have a ripple effect across the whole planet. We are here to build the New Jerusalem in consciousness by healing old wounds in ourselves and in the history that has been stuck in the bowels of the earth – a history that we can access through the underground network of the Tube.

I invite you to be a time-traveller, a Spiritourist, and come on the journey with me to prepare the way for a spiritual golden age.

Are you ready?

♪

"People get ready, there's a train a comin'
You don't need no baggage, you just get on board
All you need is faith to hear the diesels hummin'
Don't need no ticket, you just thank the Lord."

♪

"People get ready"
by Curtis Mayfield and the Impressions. 1964

Part 2

The Journey to the Depths

"O seekers, remember, all distances are traversed by those who yearn to be near the source of their being."

Kabir

Holy Spirit,

giving life to all life,

moving all creatures,

root of all things,

washing them clean,

wiping out their mistakes,

healing their wounds,

You are our true life,

luminous, wonderful,

awakening the heart

from its ancient sleep.

A prayer by Hildegard of Bingen,
German mystic

An Invitation to London

⟶

For

Rebels,

Sinners

&

Other Humans

⟶

The medieval monk and chronicler, Richard of Devizes, writing in Latin in the 1190s, gave us the following warning about the evils of London:

"When you reach England, if you come to London, pass through it quickly, for I do not at all like that city. All sorts of men crowd together there from every country under the heavens. Each race brings its own vices and its own customs to the city. No one lives in it without falling into some sort of crime. Every quarter of it abounds in grave obscenities. The greater a rascal a man is, the better a man he is accounted. .... I fear nothing for you, unless you live with evil companions, for manners are formed by association.

"Well, be that as it may! You will arrive in London. Behold, I prophesy to you: whatever evil or malicious thing that can be found in any part of the world, you will find in that one city. Do not associate with the crowds of pimps; do not mingle with the throngs in eating-houses; avoid dice and gambling, the theatre and the tavern. You will meet with more braggarts there than in all France; the number of parasites is infinite. Actors, jesters, smooth-skinned lads, Moors, flatterers, pretty boys, effeminates, pederasts, singing and dancing girls, quacks, belly-dancers, sorceresses, extortionists, night-wanderers, magicians, mimes, beggars, buffoons: all this tribe fill all the houses. Therefore, if you do not want to dwell with evildoers, do not live in London."

Thank you for accepting my invitation to the City of Sin!

Before we enter the gates to the City's underground, I want to take you on a fore-tour to contemplate London's mighty river, the Thames. The best place to do that is from one of central London's 12 public bridges. I recommend London Bridge since it is the oldest and was, for hundreds of years, the only bridge across the Thames from its first wooden construction by the Romans in 40 CE until the completion of Westminster Bridge in 1750.

From Roman times, (1st-4th century CE) the area known as Southwark on the South Bank was the sinful city of prostitution and, from Shakespeare's time, the sinful city of theatres. Disgraceful!

Yes, I can feel your disgust.

The South Bank is still the side of the river famous for arts and culture whereas the City itself on the North Bank is famous for politics, finance and business.

Prostitution is currently widespread across both banks of the river... !

Fig. 13: Drawing of London Bridge from a 1682 London Map. The spiked heads of executed criminals can be seen above the Southwark gatehouse in the foreground.

The River Thames

The name "Thames" comes from the Roman name for the river: "Tamesa" meaning "the flowing one." As you look down upon "the flowing one" from whichever bridge you are standing on, imagine a time 450,000 years BCE when the Thames Valley was populated by herders, hunters and farmers, all dependent upon the river for sacred ceremonies, drinking water, hygiene, food, transportation and defence against invaders.

The ancient ones revered the river: 215 miles long, flowing from its source in Gloucestershire out into the North Sea, it was their mystical link to the Unknown, since it flowed far beyond their horizon. Here they buried their dead, allowing the river's watery arms to carry the corpses back to the realm of the ancestors and the gods. They gave sacrifices to the river – precious items, gold, silver and the spoils of war – to make requests of the gods and to give thanks for answered prayers.

Then came the Romans in 40 CE and conquered the Celts and Druids who inhabited the shores of the Thames. The Romans established a sophisticated city, Londinium, within their stone city walls (which you can still see parts of today) and a thriving international port.

After the Romans left in 410 CE, the Angles and Saxons occupied the land. Londinium was abandoned and fell into ruin. The Saxons used the river to fish, they had a small port called Lundenwic on the strand. "The Strand" is now the name of the famous street in the city's legal and newspaper district that has taken its name from this Saxon word meaning "beach."

From 793 CE until 1066 CE there were regular Viking invasions of Britain from Norway, Sweden and Denmark.

In 1066 CE the Normans from Normandy in France, themselves the descendants of Vikings or "Norsemen," led by William the Conqueror, conquered the indigenous Saxons and also the Viking settlers at the Battle of Hastings. William ordered the construction of the Tower of London on Tower Hill at the east end of the City – a natural point of defence and fortification against any invaders who tried to enter the City by sailing in on the tides from the North Sea.

The City has not been invaded since this time, well at least not by an army or navy. There are regular "invasions" of commuters, tourists, business people, political refugees, legal and illegal immigrants and sports teams – all adding to the rich multi-cultural diversity of the City.

Fig. 14:   Tower Bridge, completed in 1894

The river has been a means of livelihood for
- Fishermen
- Merchants
- Seamen
- Slave-traders
- Navies

Down, Dirty and Divine

- Shipbuilders,
- Dockworkers
- Watermen (taxis)
- Pleasure boat companies
- Toshers – who searched through the sewage to find valuables
- Dredgers – who searched in their little rowing boats for dead bodies in order to hunt for valuables in the pockets and then get a reward for handing the body over at the nearest police station
- Mudlarks – who waited for the tide to go out and then searched through the mud on the river banks for valuable objects or anything that they could sell
- Flushers – who clean out the sewers

By 1850, during the reign of Queen Victoria, England had become the richest nation in the world. London with its many docks and huge fleet of ships had become the busiest port in the world. A quarter of a million people were living in the city and they had

Fig. 15: View of the Thames from Waterloo Bridge with Houses of Parliament and Big Ben in the background

nowhere to dump their waste except into the river. Meanwhile, contaminated water from the river was being pumped into their homes as drinking water. No surprise that diseases such as cholera and typhus were rife in the city and the death rate so high, especially amongst infants.

By 1858 the suffocating smell of sewage had infiltrated the Houses of Parliament to such an extent that it prevented the people in Parliament from breathing. It was known as "The Great Stink"! To solve the smelly problem, Joseph Bazalgette, the Chief Engineer of the Metropolitan Board of Works, designed and constructed an effective sewage system under the streets of London that is still in use today. If you join the joggers on the Victoria and Albert Embankment, you will be running on top of the sewage system as well as the District and Circle Line Tube!

Reflection

The Thames has watched the dramas of London's history play out on the stage of its riverbanks. It has watched battles and coronations, births and beheadings, joys and tragedies both private and public. Silently it has received the dead bodies of those who were murdered or killed in battle, who committed suicide or drowned accidentally. On the tides of time it has carried both prosperity and plagues in and out of London.

The river has accepted our waste, our thoughtless dumping (both human and industrial), and endeavoured to carry it out to the sea. In our human race to consume and accumulate and be free of the consequences of our actions, we have not honoured the river as the ancients once did.

The Thames has seen the best and the worst of human-beings and human-doings and flowed on, not judging but simply observing and accepting everything as it occurs. It is the Witness to the unfolding of the human story – yours and mine.

The river is our teacher.

As you enter London's underground with me on this spiritual journey, remember that you are a witness to all that came before, and all that is present now. You have the opportunity to practise detachment, observing with absolute compassion the spectres of ignorance and fear that will call to you from the underground caverns of your own soul — and the soul of London.

THE
12 CITY GATES
OF THE
NEW JERUSALEM
IN LONDON

or

THE
12 STATIONS
OF THE
COSMIC CHRIST

Station 1
LONDON BRIDGE
Alight here for
CROSS BONES CEMETERY

London Bridge Station is on the Jubilee and the Northern Line (via Bank).
Address of Site: 18-22 Redcross Way, Camberwell, Greater London SE1.
Directions to Site: Exit London Bridge Station on Borough High Street. Walk toward Southwark Street. Go past the Hop Exchange. Turn left into Red Cross Way just under the railway bridge. Cemetery is on your left. It is closed to the general public but you can still see inside from the street.

Fig.16:   Cross Bones Graveyard

"What is comes down to is this: the grocer, the butcher, the baker, the merchant, the landlord, the druggist, the liquor dealer, the policeman, the doctor, the city father and the politician – these are the people who make money out of prostitution, these are the real reapers of the wages of sin."

Polly Adler

The very place whereon I stand is holy ground. Here where I am, God is. If I mount up to heaven, God is there; if I make my bed in hell, God is there; if I "walk through the valley of the shadow of death, I will fear no evil," for God is there.

Psalm 23:4

History

Cross Bones Graveyard was a burial ground for prostitutes. It is often referred to as the Single Woman's Churchyard – a euphemism for prostitute. This area of medieval London on the south bank of the River Thames, still known today as Southwark, was famous for its brothels or "stews". The women buried at Cross Bones were known as the Winchester Geese because the Bishop of Winchester, from 1171 onwards, had the right to license the brothels in the diocese and collect the rents. Yet, when the women died, if they had not first repented, they were not considered worthy of a Christian burial and were laid to rest in this plot of unconsecrated ground.

In the 17th century this area of Southwark became very overcrowded and the graveyard was then used for the local paupers because it was cheap to be buried there. Eventually, in 1853, the cemetery was closed because the bodies were being buried too close to the surface and it had become a health hazard in the local community.

Unfortunately, the site is closed to the public today, but you can peek through the fence, which is covered with prayer ties and blessings written on ribbons, and see a statue of Mary, the Divine Mother, with some figurines of geese made of wood and porcelain.

Fig. 17: Statue of Mary inside Cross Bones with figurines of the "Winchester Geese."

Reflection

On consecrated ground

As there were no signs, the cemetery was a little difficult to find at first. I ventured into the celestial Southwark Cathedral, right opposite London Bridge station, and asked the resident archaeology expert if he knew the place. He did. Somewhat dismissively, he explained that the prostitutes were buried in this plot of unconsecrated ground whereas the cathedral was on consecrated ground.

"What constitutes 'consecrated ground'?" I asked him. Naively, maybe, I expected an explanation about ley lines crossing deep in the earth creating a particular vortex of energy that rendered a healing, uplifting effect on the people above ground - but no such thing.

"The word 'consecrated' means 'blessed and set aside for a purpose'," he said.

"Yes, but what deems the ground 'consecrated'?" I pressed.

"Oh well, the priests used to pray over the ground and I am sure they sprinkled some holy water as well," he replied.

"Is that all?" I thought, somewhat horrified, that this "consecrated ground" notion was so arbitrary. The women had gone to their deaths believing that they, and their dead offspring, were irrevocably bound for hell as a consequence of the "sinful" life they had led and, to speed the journey, they were laid to rest in unconsecrated ground – the Devil's dark domain.

Upon reflection of this information, I decided it was for me and for you to consecrate that ground, to mentally erase the notion from consciousness that there could be any place on earth where the One Omnipresent Spirit is not fully present. And if the priests and the holy men of old believed they had the authority to consecrate, then we have that same power too - if we believe it and claim it.

The act of consecrating or "making sacred" is simply based on a choice to behold a person or a thing as essentially holy. This is the true nature of being anyway, but our conscious perception of divinity raises the frequency of the being or object perceived and calls it forth in its natural perfection and wholeness.

Furthermore, Spirit is not time-bound so we can consecrate this ground retroactively and forward through time. We can neutralize any former decisions that were made about this ground that were based on ignorance rather than Truth.

On prostitution

Regarding the prostitutes, we might need to do some mental undressing of our concepts around "sin," particularly "sex as sin," and most especially "paid sex as sin."

In the human plane, the law of survival prevails. Functioning with our reptilian and mammalian brains in the driver's seat, all we can ever do is gravitate towards pleasure and happy survival while trying to avoid pain and imagined destruction.

Men are biologically programmed to scatter their seed as far and wide as they can to ensure the survival of the species. Women are biologically programmed to find a mate with strong genes who will give them strong children who will survive. Furthermore, women are driven to be impregnated by rich powerful men, men whom they can trust to take care of them while they are pregnant and nursing — a fairly full-time occupation for our cavewomen ancestresses.

Men are happy to pay for sex without the baggage of emotions, a mother-in-law, kids and a lawnmower. There is a universal law of supply and demand in operation. That, coupled with the human law of survival, means women have the power to charge men for sex!

The Winchester Goddesses — I prefer "goddesses" to "geese," and I believe they do too — were probably driven by the law of survival. They may not have known or valued their divine holy nature. It would have been difficult for them to argue against the prevailing Christian teaching that a woman's body is the occasion for sin. (According to the Catholic Encyclopedia, an occasion for sin is: *"Any person, place or thing which allures a man to sin."*)

They probably did not have access to imagining another way of life other than selling their bodies to men. Ignorance is not a crime or a sin but it does have its consequences.

Shaming and punishing women for their sexuality extends back to the Adam and Eve story in those far away years, when men were unwilling to take responsibility for their own erections or, indeed, their creative juices that spawned young offspring. Yes, it's hard to imagine that men were so immature that they preferred to blame the woman for tempting them away from a pristine relationship with God and seducing them into earthly, pleasurable indulgence.

It's even harder to imagine that a man would punish an unmarried woman for conceiving a child – as if his own penis were simply an innocent bystander. And yet harder still to believe that, having impregnated the woman, the man would besmirch her name, cast her out of the tribe for being an unmarried mother, and pass laws that would dictate what she could and could not do with her own body and with the unborn foetus that he himself had put there – maybe by penis-proxy?

So we have to pray, not just for the women who are buried at Cross Bones but also for the Bishops of Winchester and all the male customers at the brothels, especially the monks and priests who ignorantly used their god-given power to name the prostitutes "sinners" and who ignorantly judged that these women were not worthy of a Christian burial with all the imagined guarantees of a happy, relaxing afterlife listening to harps and hymns.

And on a final note... Let's not forget that Jesus' mum was an unmarried mother.

Sense of separation (sins):
blame, shame, double standards, belief in sex as sin, belief in hell

Spiritual Principles:
Love, Truth, Forgiveness, Freedom, All Life is Sacred

Prayer

There is only One Power. It is pure Love everywhere present. It lives its life as me and as everybody who is connected to my consciousness. This Divine Love suffuses every being, every soul, and every piece of earth. The very ground upon which we stand is holy since it is, and we are, birthed from the One Holy Source of Life.

I speak my Word now for this piece of ground named Cross Bones Cemetery, declaring it to be consecrated now and forever. I cast out

Down, Dirty and Divine

of consciousness any false notion about anyone or anything being any less that absolutely holy, absolutely divine, absolutely pure, absolutely untouched by the ignorant human concepts of sin and shame, evil and hell.

I speak this Word blessing all the women and children who have been buried in this piece of ground. I know that they are even now wrapped in the loving arms of the Almighty. They have never left God's side nor could they ever. And even though there is nothing to be forgiven, I declare that each sacred soul who went to their grave with any belief in guilt or sin or shame or fear, is now released from all fantasies about a punishing god or an afterlife of unending damnation.

I claim that in this moment, all these blessed beings, Goddesses, not geese, rise and fly free into their greater yet to be, unshackled by any trace of human torment, unfettered by any guilt, shame or remorse, sorrow or fear. In the name of the Most High God-Goddess, I now consecrate all these beings and name them holy, pure and innocent. This is the true nature of their essential being. I am simply stating it, convinced that it is already so.

This Word is now spoken for all women everywhere who have ever been sexually abused or incested, who have ever been cast out as a result of releasing their physical virginity before marriage or bearing a child out of wedlock, who have ever had an abortion or who have ever given a baby up for adoption as a result of social stigma and withdrawal of familial or social support. I declare that they are forgiven right now and set free from any fear or doubt about their essential purity and perfection.

Right now, by the power of this Word, I neutralize any false beliefs around sex and sexuality within men or women, any associations of sin or shame with sex, any pain or fear or guilt around the sex act, any suffering or death caused by rape or sexually transmitted *diseases. I claim and know that the high and holy purpose of sex is now being revealed in all couplings everywhere. I declare that the awareness of sex as a gift of love and pleasure, bonding and intimacy is now anchored in consciousness everywhere. I know that the possibility of sex as a direct route to Divine Ecstasy, Oneness with God in the flesh, is now embodied on earth as it already is in Heaven.*

I give thanks for the healing that has taken place here, in Cross Bones Cemetery, and everywhere in the world, through time, past present and future. I give thanks for the Omnipresent Forgiveness and release of all concepts of sin and shame around sex. I give thanks that these beloved Goddesses at Cross Bones are even now fulfilling their Divine Purpose and acting as instruments of awakening to the Truth about sex throughout the Cosmos. Though it would seem as though they had died, yet do they live, at one with the body of God/Goddess, at one with the consecrated ground of all Being.

I release my Word into Law and know that It is done, now and forever. And so It is. Amen.

Notes

Station 2
MONUMENT
Alight here for
THE MONUMENT

Monument Station is on the District and Circle Line.

Address of Site: Fish Hill Street.

www.themonument.info   Tel: 0207 626 2717.

Directions to Site: Turn right out of the Fish Hill Street exit of Monument Station. You will see the Monument ahead of you.

Fig. 18:   The Monument

> *"... when thou walkest through the fire, thou shalt not be burned; neither shall the flame kindle upon thee."*
>
> Isaiah 43:2

History

The Great Fire of London started on September 2, 1666, in a baker's shop in Pudding Lane and raged westwards across the City for the next three days until September 5. Jumping easily from one timber framed house to the next, the fire was fuelled by the winds and unchecked by the River Fleet and other rivers in the city except the Thames. Devastating the medieval City of London inside the old Roman city wall, 13,200 houses, 87 parish churches and St. Paul's Cathedral were destroyed.

The general notion at the time was that God had sent the fire to punish Londoners for their sins and, even though the city was devastated, it was seen as a cleansing - it had burned the squalid areas of the city where the bubonic plague of 1665-1666 had been rife - and also as an opportunity to rebuild.

In the wake of the Fire, King Charles II asked Christopher Wren to design and build a monument to commemorate the event. Parliament agreed it should be in Fish Hill Street, close to the site of the Great Fire's origin. Wren's Monument, completed in 1677, is a single Doric column with 311 steps inside and a viewing platform at the top for the public. The commemorative symbol on the very top is a golden urn with a flame inside. (See Fig. M in colour plate.)

Fig. 19: Pudding Lane where the Great Fire began in 1666

Down, Dirty and Divine

Why such a high column to remind Londoners of the fire? In his book "The Secret History of the World," Jonathan Black writes on page 46 that, "The Egyptians saw the obelisk as a sacred structure on which the Phoenix alights to mark the end of one civilisation and the beginning of another. An obelisk is a symbol of the birth of a new age. Like a gigantic lightning conductor, it draws down the spiritual influence of the sun."

Adrian Gilbert explains in his book "London: The New Jerusalem," on page 327, that the Phoenix is the imaginary bird from the ancient legend at the temple of Heliopolis in Egypt, dedicated to the great Sun God, Atum-Ra. Every 500 hundred years, the Phoenix would fly to Egypt from Arabia bringing the embalmed body of its parent, wrapped up to look like an egg. This egg would be placed in the Temple of the Phoenix at Heliopolis where it would catch fire. From the ashes, another Phoenix would be born.

The Monument's height of 202 feet represents the distance from the point where the fire is believed to have started. But why not a round number of 200 feet? Wren, with his understanding of sacred geometry and astronomy, knew that the height of 202 feet would create a certain length of shadow at the summer solstice of almost exactly 350 feet. The base angle of the imaginary triangle, with the Monument as its vertex, is almost 30 degrees.

If we drew a circle on the ground around the monument with a 350 feet radius, the perimeter would be 2200 feet. If we then drew a square around the monument with the same perimeter, each side would be 550 feet. Using the square base, we could construct an imaginary pyramid with its height at 350 feet, equal to the length of the shadow. The angle of the slope of this imaginary pyramid would be 51 degrees 51' which is exactly the same as the Great Pyramid of Giza. At the summer solstice, the Monument and the shadow that it casts, represents a 5/7 scale replica of the Great Pyramid!

Reflection

Even though the order in which you read these chapters is not important, as I trust you will be led to the one you need — and the world needs — at the perfect time, I recommend climbing the Monument at some point during your journey around the City's tube stations so you can get a good overview of the City from On High and pray to all the directions.

If you choose to climb all 311 steps of the Monument, you will be rewarded with a certificate when you get back to the ground floor level. Before you climb the first step you will see a metal grating over the foundations of the building. It is lit with a red lamp to symbolise the fire.

As I sat outside, after the monumental climb, and asked my Indwelling Spirit to guide me regarding the material for this chapter, I heard myself singing the song from the Disney Film Jungle Book, *"I wanna be like you."* Louie the Ape sings to Mowgli:

> *"What I desire is man's red fire*
> *To make my dream come true"*

The ape wanted to be like a human because humans had the ultimate power: the power to make a fire. In the jungle, if a human

Fig. 20:   The stair-case inside the Monument displaying the spiral pattern of sacred geometry based on Fibonacci numbers

makes a fire and the fire goes out of control, the animals die unless they can run fast enough to escape it or find refuge in a body of water. This led me to think about the power to create fire as a divine gift, something that our animal nature is not capable of and is powerless against, so it will inevitably be burned up by the flames.

Then I wondered, is that what Hell is about? i.e. having the animal nature (our humanhood) burned off so that the purity of the spirit remains? In this case, Hell is not a punishment but a cleansing fire, just like the Great Fire of London.

In Truth, there are no accidents. Everything has a cause. The cause might be due to negligence, carelessness or ignorance, but nothing happens by accident. Furthermore, nothing can occur in our experience unless it is part of the content of our consciousness. We are responsible for everything that is unfolding in our lives. In the case of every disaster, fire or otherwise, some people should have been there at the time but, for some reason, they weren't. Some people should not have been there, but they were. Some escape the flames of disaster. Some don't. I don't believe in luck.

I remember living in California in 1993 when the fires broke out along the West Coast. One of my friends, Elaine, a fellow Religious Science Practitioner, was living in Malibu and only just escaped from her home in time. She and her husband lost everything they owned but moved quickly into gratitude that they were both still alive and would start again together. Within a few days, a fellow practitioner from our spiritual community, Agape, had found them an empty house close to South Central Los Angeles and organised everything they needed to live comfortably. It was a turning point that launched them out of their comfort zone physically and spiritually.

Another friend in California lived in the hills above Laguna Beach. The fire was on its way towards her property. She asked her friends to pray. I still remember the experience of praying for her. I knew absolutely that her spirit could not and would not be touched by the flames. The next day she reported that the fire had stopped at the border of her property.

Sense of separation (sin):
fear, belief in accidents, belief in victimhood, fear of the natural elements, loss, powerlessness, death

Spiritual Principles:
One Causative Principle, Omnipotence, Immunity, Divine Right Action, Omnipresence, New Life, Power, Nothing lost in God, Transformation

Prayer

God is Omnipresence and Omni-activity, Omnipotence and Omniscience. I am that. So, too, is everyone who is joined with me in this prayer.

I declare that the fears of Hell and the fears of the eternal flames as a punishment meted out by a wrathful god are now neutralised forever. There is no god of punishment. There is only One Power that affirms every choice we make. I declare with full conviction that the concept of punishment is now healed throughout the generations, and the understanding of Truth now reigns supreme: the admission of personal responsibility and the acceptance of consequences for every thought, word and deed.

I speak this Word also for all beings who have ever deliberately started a fire with the intent to harm or destroy, all beings who have ever sentenced anyone to burn at the stake, all beings who have ever knowingly designed, built or dropped a bomb or planted a landmine, all beings who have ever mis-used the element of fire ignorantly or unconsciously. I declare that all unconscious acts have never even occurred in the mind of God for It is too pure to behold iniquity. I know therefore that the past is forgiven and released.

Down, Dirty and Divine

I declare that the awareness of the True Creative Power of the Spirit is now being awakened in each being, that awareness of the right use of all the natural elements is being cultivated in alignment with good stewardship of all the natural elements upon our precious planet.

I speak my Word for all the beings who have ever shuffled off the mortal coil as a result of fire, whether that was during the Great Fire of London or indeed any other of the many fires in the city including the fire at King's Cross Station, or a house fire, an explosion, a bomb, or at the stake. I know that their Spirits are free, alive. No one has died – in Truth.

I also speak the Word for relatives and friends, loved ones for whom there may have been a sense of loss. I accept that the Divine Love of God is the Holy Comforter and it is not bound by time. So even as this Word is spoken it goes forth and "backwards through time" as a healing balm to all those who released a loved one to the purifying flames of the Spirit. I know with absolute conviction that the Soul has never been harmed, burned or even touched.

I declare that the mighty Hand of the Divine that brings the Precious Salve of Life, where no human aid will suffice, now heals any remaining traumata from these events.

This Word of Truth now neutralizes any notions of "victim" or "tragedy." I know that each sacred soul entered the flame to be reborn. Their soul work on earth was complete and so they loosed the human coat of flesh that they might move further up the spiral of evolution.

I give thanks that the flames have burned off the dross of the past and revealed the purity of the Spirit of all those who chose this portal as their entry into the next dimension. I give thanks that Comfort and Reassurance has been offered and received and that Peace reigns supreme in the hearts of all those who have been cleansed by the Holy Flame of Spirit.

I release this Word into Law now and I allow It to be and so It is. Amen and Amen.

Notes

Station 3
BANK
Alight here for the
BANK OF ENGLAND

Bank Station is on the Central Line and the Northern Line.
Address of Site: Threadneedle Street, London EC2R 8AH.
Directions to Site: At Bank Tube Station, take exit to the Bank of England.

Fig.21:   The Bank of England

"*Lay not up for yourselves treasures upon earth, where moth and rust doth corrupt, and where thieves break through and steal: But lay up for yourselves treasures in heaven where neither moth nor rust doth corrupt, and where thieves do not break through nor steal.*"
Matthew 6:19 - 20

History

Between 1897 and 1900 the City & South London Railway (C&SLR) built Bank Tube Station next to the vaults of the Bank of England and underneath the church of St. Mary Woolnoth. The space was too congested above ground to build a proper station with an entrance and ticketing office like most London tube stations, so the entire station is located underground. The space below ground was not exactly abundant either and so, at considerable cost, a large section of the crypt of St. Mary Woolnoth's was converted into a ticketing office. So you really are standing on holy ground when you buy your ticket to ride at Bank!

The Bank of England – the central bank of the United Kingdom – was established in 1694 to act as the English Government's banker and is still the banker for Her Majesty's Government today. The headquarters have been located on London's Threadneedle Street (the capital's main financial district) since 1734. The Bank is often referred to as "The Old Lady of Threadneedle Street." It is one of the world's largest custodians of Gold Reserves: around 310 tonnes of gold bullion are held in the

Fig. 22: Bank Station ticketing hall

Down, Dirty and Divine

Vault beneath the City of London, next door to Bank Tube Station. To be opened, the Vault needs keys that are three-feet long!

In 1836, the story goes that a sewer man was doing repairs to the sewers under the Bank and found an old drain that led directly up into the bullion vaults. By removing a few floorboards he was able to haul himself up into the vault and help himself to as much bullion as he could carry, although, apparently, he was honest and did not take any gold. He did write to the Bank Directors and offer to meet them at any hour they chose to show how he got into the vault. After the meeting, in which the sewer man demonstrated his easy access to the vault, the Directors took stringent measures to make sure that all drains and sewers in and around the Bank got blocked off. The sewer man, it is said, was rewarded with a gift of £800 for his honesty.

Fig. 23: Entrance to Bank Tube Station on Threadneedle Street

Reflection

Money is a piece of metal, or a piece of paper. Sometimes it looks like a bunch of zeros on a bank statement. The zeros can be to the right of the decimal point, like this:

£.01 (= 1 penny)

or to the left of a decimal point, like this:

£1,000,000.00 (= 1 million pounds)

I heard of one New Thought teacher who fearlessly adjusted his bank statements, putting the decimal point where he wanted it, so that he could get a good visual image of what a wealthy mindset looked like on paper!

We have heard that "money is the root of all evil." Actually the correct Bible quote is: *"For the love of money is the root of all evil"* (1 Timothy 6:10.) "Love" should be translated as "attachment." You can have a negative or a positive attachment to money. You can crave it, fear it, or worship it and love it. Either way you are not free. The point is: does money have power over you? Do you believe that having it or not having it means something about you – your ability to survive, get the things you want, have fun and freedom, be attractive, be trustworthy, be loved, or be respected? Remember, money is a piece of metal or a piece of paper. It has no inherent meaning – only the meaning we choose to give it.

Anything you and I try to hold on to in the material world will eventually die or disappear. Things in the material world, including our physical bodies, are always disintegrating and decaying while other new forms of energy are being born. If you and I try to hoard money or withhold it from circulation it will eventually devalue and even disappear.

It behooves us to tap into the "inner Bank" of our own being,

Down, Dirty and Divine

which is constantly being refunded with every thought, word and deed focused on giving. Any time we try to take from another, or see him or her as the Source of our Supply instead of merely a *channel* of our Supply, we externalize our power and close our "inner Bank" from being re-filled by the Infinite Giver of Gold.

The more you and I give away from our inner Source of Supply (money, creativity, forgiveness, friendship, mercy, ideas, help, food, work), the more that money and other forms of supply show up and return to us in our world of experience.

This can sometimes be a difficult concept to grasp because we have, for so long, believed a "lie" that money is outside and needs to be acquired, earned, gotten, inherited, stolen, won by a stroke of good luck or found in order to produce feelings of power, safety, security, happiness, freedom, pleasure, comfort, ease, relaxation etc. But the feelings associated with having money are under your control and mine - just as much as any feelings or beliefs you and I may entertain about *not* having money or not having *enough* money – whatever "enough" is for you.

Sense of separation (sin):
fear of lack, poverty, lack, loss, greed, theft, selfishness, dishonesty, corruption

Spiritual Principles:
Wise Stewardship, Abundance, Inexhaustible Infinite Supply, Overflow, Givingness of God

Prayer

There is One Power. It is the Abundant Source of Infinite Supply. It fills the Universe with Itself, eternally supplying everything. It has more than enough perfect substance to support and sustain Its beloved Life in Its myriad of forms.

I AM the abundant life of God expressed. I AM abundant with ideas, thoughts, feelings, words, choices, creative gifts, dreams and possibilities – all awaiting the chance for incarnation through and as me. This is true for everyone reading this book right now and for all beings everywhere. Each of us is connected by the stream of Abundant Life that pours forth from the Infinite Source of Supply, the very creative centre of the Universe, located in perfect equal measure at every point within its Entire Holographic Self.

We are all heirs and heiresses to the abundant treasures of the Spirit, all awake now to the birth of the Christ Consciousness within our human form. As such, we are the divine recipients of gold and silver and precious gifts from all corners of the planet, far and wide.

I speak this Word now for Wisdom in the stewardship of all the financial resources of the Bank of England and all other financial institutions in the City of London and everywhere in the world.

I declare that the spiritual vibration of all the notes and coins currently in circulation is being quickened and so, as money changes hands, the essential spiritual connection between the beings involved in the interaction is surfacing in a conscious way. I call this forth NOW! I also affirm that any old dark layers of corruption, theft, fraud, embezzlement and greed are now being raised into the light of pure awareness that they may be dissolved and released.

I declare that the awareness and understanding of the Divine Quality of Abundance is now unleashed in the consciousness of the planet. I hereby neutralise, with the power of this Word, all old concepts around lack, debt, financial struggle, hardship, unemployment, loss, poverty and insufficiency. I know with certainty that the Infinite Supply of the Universe is even now revealing Its Power in and through all beings everywhere.

Down, Dirty and Divine

New creative ideas are pouring forth, new channels of income are manifesting and doors are flung wide open into new arenas of expression. Ethical ideas for raising funds and supporting life-sustaining and life-enhancing projects are now being revealed. Generosity of heart is manifesting gloriously - in expected and unexpected ways.

Financial substance is now multiplying in the experience of everyone reading this Word or connected in any way to our group consciousness. The principles of service and stewardship are now grounded and fully incarnated in all beings. The old notions of getting, taking, stealing, hoarding and cheating are now defunct. They have no more power to govern our thinking about money or about supply.

I hereby wipe out the concept of "money = security" I know that the only security is founded in the interior trust of the Eternal Givingness of Divine Supply, meeting all needs at all times with or without money. Giving and serving, sharing and circulating – these are the new laws that are now set in motion and instantaneously transforming the abundance consciousness of the planet.

I give thanks for this universal transformation of consciousness regarding our understanding and embodiment of abundance and our relationship with the divine substance known as money. I give thanks for joyous freedom around money, for creative bursts of expression that uplift the wholeness of all of us. I give thanks that the old days of struggle and poverty are over. I give thanks that there is more than enough to give and to share. I give thanks that our cup runneth over, that we dwell in Paradise together, in the flow of Infinite Wealth, as befits the Kings and Queens of Heaven.

I release this Word into Law and allow It to be. And so It is. Amen.

Notes

Station 3
BANK
Alight here for
ST. MARY WOOLNOTH CHURCH

Bank Station is on the Northern and Central Line.
Address of Site: Lombard Street, City, London EC3V 9AN.
Tel: 020 7626 9701.
Directions to Site: At Bank Tube Station, take exit no. 6.

Fig. 24: St. Mary Woolnoth Church

"None are more hopelessly enslaved than those who falsely believe they are free."

Johann Wolfgang von Goethe

History

The site of St. Mary Woolnoth has been used for worship for at least 2,000 years; traces of Celtic, Roman and Anglo-Saxon religious buildings have been discovered under the foundations.

The records state that the Christian church was built here in 1191 but, as in the case of most churches in the City of London, St. Mary Woolnoth was destroyed in the Great Fire of London in 1666. It was repaired by Sir Christopher Wren and then rebuilt by the baroque architect, Nicholas Hawksmoor, in 1716.

Reverend John Newton was the minister at St. Mary Woolnoth from 1779 until he died in 1807. He is famous for writing the hymn "Amazing Grace." His tomb was in the crypt until Bank Station bought the space for the ticketing office and the tomb was then moved to his first parish, Olney, in Buckinghamshire.

John Newton was a seaman and a slave trader. One night, in 1748, his ship got caught in a storm on the return voyage from Africa. Miraculously, all were spared but one. For Newton, this was a transformational experience that ultimately led him to enter

Fig. 25: Portrait of Rev. John Newton (1725-1807)

Down, Dirty and Divine

the ministry. For the parishioners at his prayer meetings in Olney, Buckinghamshire, he wrote the poem "Amazing Grace." In 1835 it was set to the music of a traditional song entitled "New Britain," which is the version we know today.

Amazing grace! (how sweet the sound)
That sav'd a wretch like me!
I once was lost, but now am found,
Was blind, but now I see.

'Twas grace that taught my heart to fear,
And grace my fears reliev'd;
How precious did that grace appear
The hour I first believ'd!

Thro' many dangers, toils, and snares,
I have already come;
'Tis grace hath brought me safe thus far,
And grace will lead me home.

The Lord has promis'd good to me,
His word my hope secures;
He will my shield and portion be
As long as life endures.

Yes, when this flesh and heart shall fail,
And mortal life shall cease;
I shall possess, within the veil,
A life of joy and peace.

The earth shall soon dissolve like snow,
The sun forbear to shine;
But God, who call'd me here below,
Will be forever mine.

John Newton, Olney Hymns, 1779

Ironically, a new verse was first recorded in Harriet Beecher Stowe's immensely influential 1852 anti-slavery novel "Uncle Tom's Cabin." This verse had been passed down orally in African American communities for at least 50 years before the novel's publication. It was originally one of the verses in a song entitled "Jerusalem, My Happy Home."

When we've been there ten thousand years,
Bright shining as the sun,
We've no less days to sing God's praise,
Than when we first begun.

Newton joined forces with a young man named William Wilberforce, the British Member of Parliament who led the Parliamentarian campaign to abolish the slave trade in the British Empire, culminating in the Slave Trade Act 1807.

In his diaries, Newton wrote: "I hope it will always be a subject of humiliating reflection to me, that I was once an active instrument in a business at which my heart now shudders."

Reflection

The British Empire built much of its wealth upon the slave trade – capturing slaves in Africa and transporting them via the port of London to North or South America. Today, the issue of human trafficking is one of the most pressing social problems on London's shadow side.

Perhaps this is a karmic return? One cannot expect to trade in slaves on foreign shores and not have the experience of slavery up close and personal.

We cannot enslave another human being without tying ourselves to him or her in bondage. Being a slave-owner or slave-trafficker means being enslaved. This is because we are essentially One. If you or I try to take someone else's right to freedom, then we have compromised our own.

Every soul is essentially free but, due to negative conditioning and unconscious use of our free will, we can be serving many masters – which means giving our power away to people, places and things outside ourselves.

You might ask yourself:

- What are you enslaved to?
- What do you think you cannot live without?
- Who have you taken hostage?
- Who do you control with manipulation or punishment and reward?

Perhaps it is no coincidence that the Bank of England is across the street from St. Mary Woolnoth, given that many humans on the planet right now, particularly slave-traffickers, seem to be enslaved to the money-god – or rather to the false concept of money as a symbol of power and freedom.

Sense of separation (sin):
slavery, enslavement, false sense of ownership, possessiveness, domination, cruelty, abuse

Spiritual Principles:
Freedom, Release, Grace, Mercy, Dignity, Equality, Brotherhood, Sisterhood

Prayer

There is One Power – Absolute Freedom. It is not bound to anyone, anything, any time or any space or place. Since I am born of the One Power, I am essentially free. No one and nothing can bind me without my permission, conscious or unconscious.

I am connected in consciousness to all of Life. Our relationship is one of absolute freedom. No one is slave. No one is master. All are essentially equal.

I speak this Word now for Freedom from enslavement. I know that the essential divine drive for freedom in all beings is now rising up and throwing off the shackles of oppression or domination. I declare that old thought forms, such as governments that deny basic human rights, are crumbling even as this Word is spoken.

Any organisation, institution or individual business, which is not founded on the true freedom and dignity of all beings, has no law to sustain it and is therefore falling apart. I declare that a magnificent shift in consciousness is happening right now across the planet, causing an unprecedented claiming of freedom as an inherent human right. The concepts of slavery and enslaving are now neutralised and have no more power to govern the consciousness of the people.

I declare that whatever concepts have enslaved the human race are now released. We walk free, alive, awake and aware! At choice and at Cause for our own experience.

I give thanks for this Freedom that is now established within me and throughout the world. I give thanks for the dissolution of any old limiting concepts or institutions that are based on lies. The Truth of Being has set us free.

I release this Word into the Law and know that It is done. And so It is. Amen.

Notes

Station 4
LIVERPOOL STREET
Alight here for
"BEDLAM"
(St. Mary of Bethlehem Hospital)

Liverpool Street Station is on the Central, Hammersmith & City, Circle and Metropolitan Line.

Address of Site: Liverpool Street Station

Directions to Site: Take the exit from Liverpool Street Tube Station at the corner of Liverpool Street and Old Broad Street. The graveyard of old St. Mary of Bethlehem Priory is under the current Cross Rail construction site (January 2012).

Fig. 26: Entrance to Liverpool Street Station

"Insanity: doing the same thing over and over and expecting different results."

Albert Einstein

"There is a crack in everything, that's how the light gets in."

Leonard Cohen

History

St. Mary of Bethlehem priory, located just outside the city walls at Bishopsgate, where Liverpool Street station now stands, was founded in 1247. It was the duty of the religious houses in medieval Europe to take care of the poor and needy in the local parish. Interestingly, St Mary of Bethlehem became the first "hospital" where mental patients were also housed. (The word "Bedlam" is derived from the name and has come to mean "complete chaos.")

In 1329, the priory expanded and a proper hospital was built with special sections designed to house the "weak of mind." In these dark times, people who had a mental illness would have

Fig. 27: Entrance to Liverpool Street Tube Station

Down, Dirty and Divine

been thrown out of their homes and left destitute because they were believed to be possessed of the devil. Even in the hospital the patients were treated with aversion; they were not washed or fed properly. The violent, or even not so violent, ones were kept chained to the wall. There were no humane forms of treatment. The patients were consistently ducked in freezing water as a method of trying to bring them to their senses. Otherwise, they were whipped to be punished and purged of the sins that they must have committed, and which had surely resulted in the devil possessing them?

After King Henry VIII's Dissolution of the Monasteries in 1538, the entire priory of St. Mary of Bethlehem became a mental hospital. In 1676 the hospital moved to a new location just outside Moorgate in the north of the city. It was here that the Londoners used to come for entertainment. They saw the hospital as a circus or amusement park. By the mid-eighteenth century, visitors would come in droves at the weekend for a guided tour of the "madhouse." Since the spectators paid well to be entertained and

Fig. 28: Scene of Bethlehem Hospital from William Hogarth's "A Rake's Progress." (1697 - 1764)

most of the hospital's income came from this source, the warders made sure that the patients put on a good show.

It was only towards the end of the 18th century, when King George himself became mad, that attitudes towards the insane became more respectful and the daily whipping stopped.

In 1815 the hospital was moved again to a location in Lambeth, south of the River. In 1930 another move took place to Addington in Surrey and the former Lambeth building was turned into the Imperial War Museum.

Reflection

One night, shortly after I began the work on this chapter, I had a dream in which I saw an image of a man with no teeth except one in the top row at the front of his mouth. He looked like a medieval gargoyle in the Temple Church. He was wearing a blindfold and a loose white night shirt. He had thin brown greasy hair and he was unshaven. He had a cry of agony on his face. This image has not left me. As more of the picture was revealed, I knew he was an inmate in Bedlam and he was being used for entertainment. The crowds were jeering at him, taunting him, and even throwing cold water on him. He pissed in fear, which made them laugh all the harder.

I realised later that these humiliation tactics used at Bedlam are similar to our current methods of torturing people in prison to extract a confession. Sadly, the human psyche has the capacity to use power over others in an abusive way, stripping humans of their essential dignity, manipulating them with mental, emotional or physical torture in order to win at the game of self-preservation.

Have you ever suffered from madness – your own or somebody else's? Have you ever

a) felt that you were losing your mind?

b) been trapped by paranoia?

c) been driven by addiction?

d) indulged in obsessive compulsive behaviours or

e) fallen into depression?

Have you ever taunted, ridiculed, bullied or shunned anybody who suffered from mental illness, senility, Alzheimers or anybody who was simply less able than you?

How often do you call yourself an idiot?

a) When you forget something?

b) When you are not perfect?

c) When you don't do something the way you think you should have done it according to someone else's standards or expectations – perhaps your parents' or your spouse's?

How often do you call someone else an idiot?

a) When they behave differently from you?

b) When they have different religious or political views?

c) When they don't come up to your high standards of intelligent functioning in society?

Do you ever talk to yourself? Eckhart Tolle, author of "The Power of Now," tells the story of how he began talking to himself when he was alone and didn't think anything of it until he witnessed a man talking to himself in public and judged him as insane. It was then that he realized, with humility, that he had the same madness only he had not reached the point of talking to himself unknowingly in public.

In her book "The Dark Side of the Light Chasers," Debbie Ford tells the story of a man who kept calling others idiots because he could not accept the idiot in himself. When she questioned him, it turned out that he had done something as a child that caused others to laugh at him and he vowed never to do or say anything stupid again. This aspect of himself that he had denied caused him to attract "idiots" into his life in large numbers. It was his psyche's method of begging to be seen, accepted and set free.

Have you ever repeated an action believing it would turn out differently from all the other times before?
  a) Fallen in love and expected to live in romantic fantasy land forever?
  b) Gone out drinking and expected not to get drunk?
  c) Worked out after a long break and expected to be pain-free?
  d) Eaten junk food every day and expected not to feel sluggish or put on weight?

"Bedlam" meant chaos.
Where is your life chaotic or unmanageable?
  a) In your relationships?
  b) At work?
  c) In your home?
  d) Financially?
  e) Around time-keeping?

Phew! Now breathe a sigh of relief that you might well qualify as insane, but at least you are not alone! We are all in this together, learning to behold self and others with the Mind of the Divine.

Sense of separation (sin):
insanity, false identity, ridicule, mockery, cruelty, chaos

Spiritual Principles:
Omniscience, Sanity, Sound Mind, Love, Understanding, Compassion

Prayer

There is One Power, it is the All-Knowing Mind – Omniscience. It is present at every point within Itself. The sound Mind of the Divine is present in and through every cell of creation. This Mind knows only Wholeness and Perfection. This Mind includes every manifestation of Itself, within Itself. This Mind beholds Itself with Love and Acceptance, Compassion and Mercy. It could not do otherwise. There is no judgment in the Mind of God.

The Mind of the Divine lives, moves and has Its being in, as and through me. I am One with the Infinite Creator, that same Mind which created the entire universe. As such I am One with the Perfect Mind of all beings everywhere.

I now speak this Word for all those beings who once played or now play the role of "patient" at the St. Mary of Bethlehem hospital, plus all those who made their transition in the hospital and are now buried in the priory graveyard at Bishopsgate. I declare for and about them, that they were, are now, and always will be the pure and perfect creations of the Whole Mind of the One. I know that they are part of the Divine Creation and are therefore made in the image and likeness of Divine Intelligence. I know that any and all appearances of insanity are now neutralised by the power of this Word. I call forth the Soundness of Mind functioning in and as all beings now.

I now speak this Word for the wardens, doctors, monks and nuns who tended to the patients at St. Mary of Bethlehem hospital. I declare that any sense of separation between patient and doctor or patient and warden is now dissolved. I affirm that all false judgments are now released; all ignorant attitudes that triggered dehumanizing forms of treatment are now wiped out in the spirit of true awareness – the awareness of our essential Oneness and our dignity as emanations of the Divine. All that is real is the love and peace that flowed back and forth, and flows back and forth, between the staff and the patients.

I further cast out of consciousness any concept of disorder or chaos. I know that the Mind of the Divine is eternally ordered and serene.

I speak my Word for all those who came to be entertained by the patients at St. Mary of Bethlehem and declare "Peace! Be still!" to any old desire to mock or ridicule an appearance of insanity or mental weakness. All false attempts to kill, hide, lock away, punish or mock any aspect of ourselves, which we preferred not to own or identify with, are now surrendered. The eye of God cannot behold iniquity in anything that It has made; simply, It has made everyone and everything.

And as this Word is spoken specifically for all those who were drawn to the St. Mary of Bethlehem hospital, it is also spoken generally for all psychiatric wards, all mental hospitals and all patients and staff in any institution or home in any location and in any time period on the planet Earth.

I declare that the Sound Mind of the Divine now reveals itself in and through all beings. I declare that Peace and Love now infuse the walls of these places and the relationships amongst the people who are staying or working in them. "Peace be still and know that I AM!" is the instantaneous healing Word to all who have the appearance of a troubled spirit. "Peace! Be still!" is the Word that calms and restores, aligns and comforts. "Peace! Be Still!" is the divine ordination to remember what is true and to rest in the gentle mercy of the Everlasting Arms.

I give thanks that this Word has been spoken, that all false judgments around what seems to be "mad," in self and others, have now fallen away. I give thanks for the revelation of the Divine Intelligence, Divine Wholeness and Divine Peace in those who have been deemed mad and those who have been called to tend to them. I give thanks for the dissolution of any trauma caused by ignorance, any pain caused by unconsciousness. I give thanks for the omni-active awareness of the Spirit now operating through mind and body of all beings everywhere, for the unconditional acceptance of all manifestations of the One, honouring each soul as the perfect holographic image of the Divine.

I release my Word into Law and I allow It to be. And so It is. Amen.

Notes

Station 5
BLACKFRIARS
Alight here for
ST BRIDE'S CHURCH

Blackfriars Station is on the Circle Line and the District Line.
Address of Site: Off Fleet Street, London EC4Y 8AU.
www.stbrides.com   Tel: 020 7427 0133.
Directions to Site: From Blackfriars, walk into the City and turn left into St. Bride's Lane. Go left up the steps into St. Bride's Avenue and turn left into the church gates.

Fig. 29:   An early Printing Press. This woodcut from 1568 shows the left printer removing a page from the press while the one at the right inks the text-blocks.

"For by thy words thou shalt be justified, and by thy words thou shalt be condemned."

Matthew 12:37

Fig. A. Hell in Islam. (See Fig. 1)

Fig. B. Greek icon of the Second Coming. (See Fig.11)

Fig. D. Lamb of God, emblem of the Crusades. (See Fig. 9)

Fig. C. The New Jerusalem, showing the 12 City Gates and the Lamb (Christ) in the centre. (See Fig. 10)

Fig. E. The Dome of the Rock, Islamic Shrine, Jerusalem. (See Fig. 6)

Fig. F. *Way Out sign on Underground platform*

Fig. G. *Famous symbol of the Underground*

Fig. I. *Mural of Dick Whittington (See Fig. 62.)*

Fig. H. *Famous warning on Underground platforms*

Fig. J., Fig. K., Fig. L. *Gargoyles from Temple Church*

Fig. M. Symbol of the Great Fire – the flame in the urn atop The Monument

Fig. O. Decoration on entrance gate to St. Mary Woolnoth. Symbol of crossed swords pointing upwards means readiness to fight evil.

Fig . N. Symbol of Truth and Justice atop the Old Bailey

Fig. Q. Statue of Queen Boudicca, Westminster

Fig. P. 14th century crypt chapel in St. Bride's, the journalists' church

Fig. R. Mary blessing the Winchester Geese in Cross Bones Cemetery

Fig. S. St. Paul's Cathedral with small version of The Monument in foreground

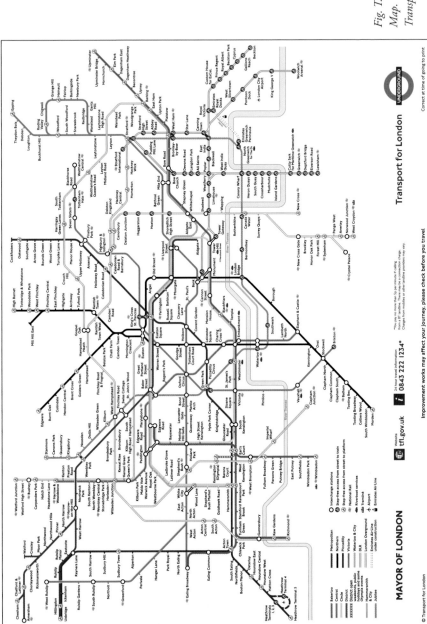

Fig. T. Beck's Underground Map. Printed courtesy of Transport for London.

History

St Bride's is famously known as the Journalist's Church, partly for its location in Fleet Street, the original home of the British newspaper, and partly for the fact that Wynkyn de Worde, assistant to William Caxton (first to use the printing press in England), moved his commercial press to the St. Bride's churchyard in 1500. Other printers and bookbinders set up their businesses nearby. As a result, St Bride's became a leader in the distribution of the printed word.

The font in which the famous London diarist, Samuel Pepys, was baptized in 1633, stands in the church to this day. On the left of the main altar there is a special memorial altar for all nationalities of journalists who either died naturally, or in a war zone, while fulfilling their mission to communicate first hand to the world about local or global conflict situations.

St. Brides stands on a Celtic site of worship. There was a clear water spring here, at the east end of the church, which was dedicated about 2000 years ago to Brigit or Brighde, the Celtic goddess of healing, childbirth and fire. The well was still supplying water until the 19th century but has since been covered over.

In the sixth century a Christian church was built on the same piece of ground and dedicated to St. Bridget, an Irish saint, often associated with watery places. In total, eight churches have been built on this site.

After the Great Fire of London in 1666, St. Brides was rebuilt by Sir Christopher Wren, the architect who designed the steeple – the highest in London at that time. It is said that the steeple inspired a baker on nearby Ludgate Hill to design the tiered wedding cake that has become a tradition at weddings around the world.

If you move downstairs into the crypt, you will see an exhibition of the church's history and the evidence in stone of the different influences over this church: Romans, Danes, Normans etc. There is a small peaceful chapel at the far end of the crypt dedicated to writers. With a uniquely designed altar piece bearing images of quills and gothic manuscripts, one of the eight seats, carved out of the ancient stone wall of the chapel, is waiting for you to sit and reflect.

Fig. 30:   14th century crypt of St. Bride's – Altar in Writers' Chapel (see Fig P. in colour section)

Fig. 31:   Semi-circular stone seat in St. Bride's crypt chapel.

Down, Dirty and Divine

Reflection

Let's activate our Divine Potential and live in the vision of a transformed world while we are at St. Bride's. Imagine it is 2025, the year when Alice Bailey predicted the Second Coming. From this vantage point of awakened consciousness, let's reflect back on that pivotal year in our human evolution: 2012.

Remember a time when not all speakers and writers were in integrity with their Divine essence, when they used the power of language to lie about facts or to assassinate character or even to sentence to death. Remember when newspaper editors were dominated more by the financial pressures to sell than a calling to inform and communicate world events; when it was acceptable to publish negative gossip, sensationalised stories of the personal or secret lives of celebrities, focusing on sex scandals, tragedies, violent conflicts; when stories of terror and destruction such as war or natural disasters were used to entertain; when this kind of life-alienating reporting only sold because there was a readership which was hungry for it and which proved its appetite in cash. We were that readership.

While you and I were living under the law of self-preservation, we probably used our divine gift of the Word in ways that were less than life-enhancing. We lied, we gossiped, we blamed, we embellished, we swore, we criticized, we broke our promises, we condemned, we denied, we slandered, we spat.... All this out of ignorance. And, in the process, harming ourselves as much as, or more than, we harmed each other. Thank God those days are over!

Let us also reflect upon the English language itself – officially the international language, but composed of so many language influences such as Celtic, Latin, Saxon, Viking, Norman French, Italian, Flemish and Welsh. England, and especially London, has always been a magnet for invaders and traders and each culture has made their contribution to the English language. Similarly the

British Crown has colonized large parcels of land across the world in India, Africa, America, Canada, Australia, New Zealand, and Ireland with the result that English is now spoken ubiquitously and taught in schools as the first language or the first foreign language.

When I went to study for the ministry in the USA in 1989, I thought communication in English would be the least of my problems. How naieve!! One morning after church, I was having a conversation with an elderly congregant over coffee. I thought she was fully engaged in what we were discussing. She seemed to be hanging on my every word. I asked her a question. She didn't answer. She was still hanging. Then, a little flustered, she replied, "Oh honey, I didn't understand one word of what you were saying - I have just been enjoying your accent!" She smiled happily as though that was completely OK...

It was a lesson for me that English is spoken in as many different ways as there are people speaking it. Just like the Divine is perceived in as many different ways as there are life-forms interpreting It/Her/Him.

Sense of separation (sin):
lies, falsehoods, gossip, slander, violation, misuse, sensationalism, exaggeration

Spiritual Principles:
Truth, Clarity, Communication, Understanding, Creative Power of the Word, Transparency

Prayer

There is only One Power, the Creative Word of God. I AM the offspring of the Word, created by the Divine in Its own image and likeness. I AM the Word made flesh. This is true for all beings everywhere, each one seeded by the Divine Word, each one a living manifestation of the Creative Power of the Infinite. I know that I

Down, Dirty and Divine

am joined in the sacred family of humankind with all my brothers and sisters throughout the universe. We are inseparable and so this Word goes forth as Truth for all beings.

I speak this Word now and know that I am setting new Law in motion. From this point forth, the words that are spoken or written, heard or thought, through and as me, are formed in Truth bringing life, hope, comfort, clarity and love into expression for the upliftment of the Whole.

For me, and all those who have laboured under the lies of their conditioning, their history, their religion, their culture, their ancestral past, this Word acts as a sword of Truth and dissolves the veil of separation. The authentic Divine essence is called forth now from within me and from within all beings in all of Its shining glory.

The Divine Word now quickens the life of the media revealing its holy purpose to communicate Truth. This includes every journalist, copywriter, advertiser, photographer, newspaper business, magazine business, newscaster, TV station, author, editor, proof-reader, publisher, book distribution company – indeed any individual or organization that are bearers of the Word. The Divine Word of Truth now pervades the Internet and all forms of technology used for communication. The Divine Word is Omnipresent always communicating harmoniously, joyously, clearly, truthfully to reveal the sacred connection that joins all of Creation, to remind us of Who we are.

I speak this Word for all journalists who have made their transition to the other side of the Veil in the course of their duty either reporting from war zones or being murdered as a means of being silenced. I bless Marie Colvin and Remi Ochlik and all these souls for their contribution to humanity and know that their words and images of Truth live on as testimony to their courage and honesty. They are immortal just as the Word is immortal too.

Furthermore, I accept that the English language, as the

international medium for communication, is now free of any vestiges of imperialism, exploitation or domination. I know that English is taught and learned in a conscious way and in an atmosphere of joy and expansion. I am declaring that English, along with all other languages spoken by the peoples of the earth, is simply the channel for the language of the heart, the language of peace, understanding and unity, and furthers the development of humankind as a whole.

I declare that Spirit speaks and writes through and as me, now and forever, and I rest in the knowledge that Its Word is Whole and can only birth blessings that multiply after their own kind.

I give grateful thanks that this Word has gone forth. I give thanks that the entire media world has been transformed and is now governed by Truth. I give thanks that the use of English as the international language is now the medium for peace, understanding and unity.

I now release this Word into Law and know that It is done and so It is. Amen.

Notes

Station 6
ST. PAUL'S
Alight here for
THE OLD BAILEY

St. Paul's Station is on the Central Line.

Address of Site: Central Criminal Court, Old Bailey, EC4M 7EH.
www.oldbaileyonline.org.   Tel: 020 7248 3277.

Directions to Site: Take exit 2 from St. Paul's Tube Station. Turn left on to
Newgate Street and walk towards Holborn. Turn left into Old Bailey. The Old
Bailey Central Criminal Court is on the corner of Old Bailey and Newgate
Street with the main entrance on Old Bailey.

Fig. 32:   The Old Bailey Courthouse on the site of the old Newgate Prison

*"Judge not according to the appearance, but judge righteous
judgment."*

John 7:24

History

The Old Bailey has been London's principal criminal court for centuries. The unusual name means "fortified wall." Old Bailey is the road that follows the line of the old fortified Roman wall of the City of London.

The original medieval courthouse was first built in the 16th century thanks to a generous financial gift from Sir Richard Whittington, Mayor of London. The courthouse was right next door to the infamous Newgate Gaol (see next chapter) so it was very convenient to try the accused, sentence them to gaol and, if they had committed a capital offence, execute them in the Hanging Yard behind the courthouse. In medieval England there were 150 capital offences, including petty theft.

From 1783 to 1868, condemned prisoners were hanged in full view of the waiting public. They would be led from their cells along Dead Man's Walk to the gallows, in what is today's Warwick Square, behind the Old Bailey. If the families did not claim the body to bury it themselves, the corpses would have been buried in a lime pit in the vicinity. It is said that many were buried in the Walk itself. (If you walk back towards St. Paul's along Newgate Street, you can turn right into Warwick Lane and right again into Warwick Square and see the old courtyard although it is closed to the public.)

The old prison building was knocked down in 1902 and construction began on the current Old Bailey courthouse building, which was opened in 1907 on the site of Newgate prison. Notice the beautiful dome that reflects the famous dome of nearby St. Paul's Cathedral. Atop the dome stands the golden figure of Justice with a sword in her right hand and a pair of scales in her left. (See Fig. N in colour section.) Today the Court hears cases from the City of London and the Greater London area and those remitted to it from England and Wales.

There are two aspects of the history of the Old Bailey that I have been guided to address in this chapter: sexism and racism.

Sexism

Can you believe that there used to be different laws for women and men? Preposterous, eh? The suffrage movement began campaigning in 1866 to get votes for women and the right to run for political office. After all, men who owned property had been entitled to vote from 1832 and working class men got the right to vote in 1867.

Thank Goddess for Emmeline Pankhurst, her daughter, Christabel, and also Emily Davison who had the courage to speak up and lead campaigns to expose and eliminate discriminatory practices against women in law, politics and society.

In 1905 the suffrage movement turned militant. Emmeline and Christabel Pankhurst staged demonstrations and got arrested.

According to Paula Bartley in her book "Emmeline Pankhurst," Ms Pankhurst told the court during her 1908 trial: *"We are here not because we are law-breakers; we are here in our efforts to become law-makers."*

Fig. 33: Emmeline Pankhurst

Emily Davison was tried at the Old Bailey in 1912 and Emmeline Pankhurst in 1912 and again in 1913. Pankhurst, and other women who were imprisoned, staged hunger strikes. They were force-fed through tubes so that they would not starve to death and create bad press for the government.

Victory came in 1918 when women over the age of 30 were finally given the vote - but only if they were married! In 1928 women were finally given the vote on the same terms as men.

Racism

On 3rd January, 2012, Stephen Lawrence's murderers were on trial in the Old Bailey. Stephen Lawrence had been stabbed to death at a bus stop in London in April, 1993, when he was only 18. It was a racist attack by a group of white youths but they were not brought to trial until 19 years later due to the mismanagement of the case in, what was then, an institutionally racist police force. A very critical report of the way the case was handled in 1999 initiated a review of racist attitudes amongst the police and greater awareness in dealing with similar cases.

Directly after the trial there were complaints that the murderers' sentences were too short. One of the men was 17 and the other 16 when they murdered Stephen and so they were sentenced as though they were juveniles. Their sentences would have been 30 years if they had been 18 or over at the time of the murder.

Reflection

It is reassuring to know that we don't have to police the universe. There is a Divine Justice in this universe, regardless of what may happen in the Law Courts. The judges and the lawyers may do their best to mete out justice, but whatever they think say and do, Divine Justice will prevail. Everyone will get what they believe they deserve. The Law of the Universe cannot dish up anything other than that.

Judgment follows consciousness

So in an ignorant society where the belief is that death is the punishment for "sin" (whatever "sin" is determined to be), executions will occur.

In an ignorant society where the prevailing belief is that men are entitled to rights and power by dint of their genitals, women will be suppressed if they try to take power for themselves.

In an ignorant society where the prevailing belief is that one race is superior to another, the "superior" race will do what it has to, to maintain power over the "inferior race", including killing. This is the race for survival, or in other words, the human race.

The Stephen Lawrence case – an alternative perspective

When I saw the journalists outside the Old Bailey on January 3, 2012, they were like hungry wolves, unperturbed by the rain and cold, salivating for a picture that would create a sensation.

After seeing the journalists, I decided to move on with my research but, an hour later, I happened to pass an office building in a different part of the City with a TV in the reception area showing pictures of Stephen Lawrence's murder trial. I marvelled at how fast technology relays information. Two days later I switched on my computer and a news report about the trial presented itself to me on the Yahoo homepage!

Knowing that there are no accidents or coincidences, I realized that the soul of Stephen might be trying to get through to me – perhaps so that the story can be told differently?

Let us look at the possibility that behind the appearance of this very human tragedy, a greater cosmic drama might be playing itself out. Is it possible that Stephen and his attackers had a pact before they came to earth? Did the attackers agree to be the bad guys and did Stephen agree to die as an innocent martyr? Interestingly, all the boys were in their teens. This must have been part of the agreement. When young people behave with such grotesque cruelty towards one another, we are compelled to look at the causes and conditions in which they learned to hate.

We have a choice: to level our hate at the murderers and our sympathy at Stephen and his parents – or to honour them all as grand and glorious, birthless and deathless beings, who made a pact to expose racial hatred and to wait nearly 20 years before the Truth would come to light – at a time when the consciousness of the masses was awake enough to say "This kind of racism in our police force and legal institutions is no longer acceptable."

As humanity wakes up and enough people join in agreement that the death penalty as well as sexist and racist laws are unacceptable, the law of the land must change too. The body of human law can only reflect the internal shifts in our own consciousness. And the internal shifts in our own consciousness are the midwives to the birth of social change.

I offer up my tribute to Emmeline Pankhurst and Stephen Lawrence and all of the other heroines and heroes who gave their lives in the cause of justice and freedom, who suffered that we might awaken.

Sense of separation (sin):
racism, sexism, false judgement, barbarism, corruption, prejudice

Spiritual Principles:
Justice, Divine Law, Equality, Righteous Judgement, Balance, Wisdom

Prayer

There is only One Power. It is the Law that governs the Universe. It sustains all of Life in perfect Balance and Harmony. It is Just, It is Perfect, It is Eternal and it is True. It can never compromise Itself or go out of integrity with Itself. It is 100% consistent, unchanging and reliable, constantly revealing on the outer what is seeded on the inner levels of consciousness.

I am another way that the Word has been made flesh through the Divine Activity of the Universal Law. My life is governed by the Laws that govern the entire universe. I am one with the Life of all beings everywhere. The Law governs my goings out and my comings in. It sustains my mind, my body and my being in perfect balance and harmony.

I declare that the Law of Divine Justice that governs the universe is now being revealed in all legal cases past present and future. Even as I speak this Word, I declare that an opening is taking place in consciousness, a surrender and an allowing for the Divine Law to have full sway in mind, in body and in the body of affairs of every sacred soul, every organisation, institution and law court upon the planet. Something magnificent is taking place here. The old human laws of survival, fear and limitation are crumbling into the nothingness from whence they came and the Law of Right-Use is having its way in the consciousness of the people. I know that laws that appeared as racist or sexist, or in any way biased towards a cherished point of view, are now neutralised. They no longer have power to sustain themselves because they are not built upon Truth.

I declare that all seemingly unjust sentences are now healed by the hand of Divine Justice. Any sentences that were passed in ignorance of Truth are now being reversed. I declare that Divine Restitution is upon us and everything that was ever thought, said or done that was out of alignment with the Law of the Universe is now restored by the Sword of Truth. I declare that the fight is over.

I give thanks that the Law of the Universe is established within me and within all beings. I give thanks that the work of every court of law across the world is now guided by Divine Justice. Every lawyer, every lawmaker, every court clerk, every judge, every jury is now undergirded, sustained and maintained by this power of the Divine Law. I give thanks that Harmony reigns supreme.

I release this Word into the outworking of the Universal Law and know that it is done. And so It is. Amen.

Notes

Station 6
ST. PAUL'S
Alight here for
NEWGATE PRISON

St. Paul's Station is on the Circle Line.

Address of Site: Newgate Street at Old Bailey.

Directions to Site: Take exit 2 from St. Paul's tube station. Follow signs to Old Bailey. Turn left on to Newgate Street and walk towards Holborn. Just before you get to the street Old Bailey, you will see the plaque commemorating Newgate Prison on the wall of the current Central Criminal Court (Old Bailey).

Fig. 34:   Plaque commemorating site of Newgate Prison where the Old Bailey now stands

"We are all doing time."

Bo Lozoff

"Stone walls do not a prison make,
Nor iron bars a cage"

Richard Lovelace

History

Dating back to 1188, Newgate Gaol was housed in the gatehouse of the New Gate – one of the fortified entrances to the City of London in the Roman Wall.

In 1423, with money left by Lord Mayor Richard Whittington, the prison was rebuilt and enlarged. However, for most of its existence, the prison was a damp dark dungeon underground. Mass murderers were thrown in together with petty thieves and innocent victims. Food consisted of bread and water. The cells were not cleaned. There were no proper toilets. Usually prisoners died of malnutrition and disease, especially "gaol-fever", as typhus was commonly called. Wardens could be bribed to provide extras that would make life more bearable, like food or alcohol. Ironically, if the prisoners had enough money, they could pay to get out!

From 1196 – 1783 those who had received the death sentence were taken to Tyburn gallows to be hanged. (See next two chapters.)

Starting in 1787, due to overcrowding at Newgate, approximately 160,000 prisoners were shipped out to Botany Bay in New South Wales, Australia to found a new penal colony. For many it was an alternative to hanging and they had a chance to live – if they survived the long sea voyage.

From 1783 until 1868 there were public hangings outside Newgate/The Old Bailey. Executions continued behind closed doors until 1902 when the prison was demolished and the Old Bailey (Central Criminal Court) expanded over the site.

Elizabeth Fry, the famous Prison Reformer, began entering the prison in the early 19th century. She was concerned that women prisoners were being forced into prostitution and that the prisoners' children were not getting educated. She started a school for these children and had the flogging of women prisoners abolished in 1820.

The book, "Moll Flanders" (1722) by Daniel Defoe includes

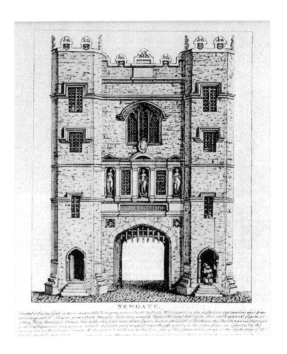

Fig. 35:   Old Newgate Prison, which was replaced in 1777

scenes from Newgate prison that Defoe was able to write from first hand experience having been sent there in 1702 because of a pamphlet he wrote attacking the government.

In order to see a typical Newgate cell you can visit the Viaduct Tavern opposite the former prison at 126 Newgate Street. (Tel: 020 7600 1863.) If the pub is not too busy, the owners will take you down the narrow curving staircase into the cellar. The old cell is now used as a cold storage room. It is spine-chillingly cold...

Reflection

On crime
Can you imagine a time when there was such poverty and desperation that people would steal a loaf of bread in the full

Fig. 36: A typical old Newgate cell as seen in the basement of the Viaduct Tavern opposite the former prison.

knowledge that if they were caught they would be sent to jail and hanged? Can you imagine such overwhelming hunger that the instant gratification of satisfying the appetite outweighed the horrific consequences of the act? The consequences of breaking the law are no longer as severe but has the mad ego really changed? The mad ego is the voice that says, "I think I can get away with it" not caring if another is harmed in the process. We are then imprisoned by the karmic reaction to the act, compelled to experience the harm that we have caused.

On mental prisons

We have all had our own sense of limitation, stuckness, imprisoned by our own thoughts that we have recycled obsessively until they have become the law of our lives: trapped by a job that is less than we are capable of, trapped by a mortgage, trapped in a marriage, trapped by an unwanted pregnancy, trapped by a legal situation.

None of these traps are real, although they certainly feel real. Fortunately, the trap is in our thinking and what we have once thought, we can now "un-think" if it no longer serves us.

A personal story

While I was growing my ministry in South Africa, a woman came to me for counselling. She was on the run from the police. I suggested that she consider giving herself up. At first she looked at me as if I was insane. And then a peace came over her. That night she surrendered and became willing to hand herself in.

The very next day she was caught and arrested and sentenced to eight years that might be reduced to three years for "good behaviour."

Prison was a shock. The most humiliating experience was not having any privacy. After an initial period of adjustment to the new regime, she courageously decided to use her time in prison to grow spiritually. Her husband brought her metaphysical course books to her and she spent many hours alone in silent reflection. Through her studies, her contemplation and her self-examination, she went deep in her inner relationship with God.

When I went to visit her, she looked 20 years younger, was filled with joy and gratitude and had a radiance that I have seldom witnessed. She thanked me for suggesting that she give herself up because that was her turning point. In that moment she stopped running and became free.

Sense of separation (sin):
imprisonment, powerless, bondage to old concepts, stealing, crime, fear

Spiritual Principles:
Freedom, Omnipotence

Prayer

There is One Power, Omnipotent Spirit. It is pure Freedom. It is the All in All. It cannot be trapped bound or limited in any way.

There is nothing other than God, no one other than God. God created me in Its own image and likeness. It created me free! I am the daughter of Freedom, a free Spirit. No mental or material prison walls can ever contain me.

I know that I am one with everyone who is connected to my consciousness, including all the prisoners who spent part of their earth journey at that institution called Newgate, and any person who has ever been behind bars, whether rightly or wrongly, and anyone who has ever felt imprisoned by a relationship, a situation or a thought or an emotion. I bless all political prisoners, all prisoners of war, all those who have been imprisoned for their beliefs and have undergone any kind of torture or punishment or deprivation from their gaolers.

I declare that Spirit now flows through every gaol upon this planet, dissolving the thought forms of lawbreaking or imprisonment. I speak my word for all beings everywhere declaring that the shackles of humanhood are now released! Any old attachment to the human realm is now dissolved.

I know that the Spirit of all beings cannot and will not be contained by metal bars or by brick walls, whether they be material or mental.

I declare now that all are pardoned. All are forgiven for the ignorant belief that they were trapped, that they were criminals. No son or daughter of God could ever or would ever commit a crime. I declare that the old notion of crime has now become defunct. I declare that the sons and daughters of the most High dwell together in holy community where Freedom reigns supreme!
I give thanks for Freedom being established on earth as it is in

Heaven. I give thanks for the appearances of suffering and pain from the past due to any form of imprisonment, now being lifted. I give thanks for healing that is taking place in prisons around the planet right now. No one is trapped in victimhood. Everyone is divinely self aware, at cause for all their actions and reactions and, thereby, free.

I release this Word into Law and I allow It to be. And so It is. Amen.

Notes

Station 6
ST. PAUL'S
Alight here for
ST. SEPULCHRE CHURCH
and the walk from
NEWGATE TO TYBURN

St Paul's Station is on the Central Line.
Address of Site: The Church of St. Sepulchre without Newgate,
10 Giltspur Street, London EC1A 9DE.
www.st-sepulchre.org.uk.   Tel: /Fax: 020 7248 3826.
Directions to Site: Take exit 2 from St. Paul's Tube Station. Follow signs to Old
Bailey. Turn left on to Newgate Street and walk towards Holborn. Cross the
road at the corner of Newgate Street and Old Bailey. You will see St. Sepulchre
Church diagonally opposite the Old Bailey building.

Fig. 37:   St. Sepulchre without Newgate Church

*"Judge not, and ye shall not be judged: condemn not, and ye shall
not be condemned: forgive, and ye shall be forgiven."*

Luke 6.37

"When are we like God? I will tell you.
In so far as we love compassion and practice it steadfastly,
to that extent do we resemble the heavenly Creator
who practices these things ceaselessly in us."

Mechtild of Magdeburg

History

Originally, there was a Saxon Church on this site dedicated to St Edmund the King and Martyr. During the Crusades to the Holy Land in the 12th century, it was renamed "St. Edmund and the Holy Sepulchre" in reference to the Church of the Holy Sepulchre in Jerusalem – the site of Jesus' tomb. The name eventually became abbreviated to St. Sepulchre. In 1671, having been damaged by the Great Fire of 1666, the church was rebuilt by Sir Christopher Wren.

The focus of this section is on St. Sepulchre's role in ministering to the condemned prisoners at Newgate Gaol – particularly on the day of an execution.

The tradition started in 1605, when a St. Sepulchre Bellman would go over to the prisoner's cell at Newgate at midnight on the execution day. He would ring twelve double tolls on the Execution Bell to rouse the prisoner (in case s/he was sound asleep!) Then he delivered, with an audible voice, the lines of the rhyme below:

"All you that in the condemned hole do lie,
Prepare you, for tomorrow you shall die.
Watch all, and pray: the hour is drawing near
That you before the Almighty must appear.
Examine well yourselves, in time repent
That you may not to eternal flames be sent,
And when St. Sepulchre's Bell in the morning tolls,
The Lord above have mercy on your souls."

"Macbeth" was completed by Shakespeare in 1606, a year after the tradition started with the Bellman. He is alluded to in Lady Macbeth's speech:

"It was the owl that shrieked, the fatal bellman,
Which gives the stern'st goodnight."

The hand-bell is now displayed under glass in the church to the south of the nave.

An execution was major entertainment in medieval London. Once the hangings stopped at Tyburn Tree in 1783 and were carried out at Newgate, huge crowds gathered in St. Sepulchre's churchyard and in the area around the prison, even sleeping on the streets the night before to be sure of reserving a good spot where they could get the best view of the action.

The growing and very rowdy crowds made it impossible for the priests and the bellman to make the short walk across the road

Fig. 38: St. Sepulchre Bellman's handbell

to Newgate in order to reach the prisoner and prepare her/him for the execution. After an accident outside the prison in 1807 when a number of spectators were crushed to death, a secret tunnel was built from St. Sepulchre's that led under the road and directly to the Newgate cells. The top part of the archway leading into the tunnel is visible on the inside south wall of the church, but the tunnel itself has been sealed off and is no longer accessible from this side or the other side in the basement of the Old Bailey.

Fig. 39: The boarded up arch over the former secret tunnel which led from St. Sepulchre to the Newgate cells

The Walk from Newgate to Tyburn

"Oranges and lemons" say the Bells of St. Clement's
"You owe me five farthings" say the Bells of St. Martin's
"When will you pay me?" say the Bells of Old Bailey
"When I grow rich" say the Bells of Shoreditch
"When will that be?" say the Bells of Stepney
"I do not know" say the Great Bells of Bow
"Here comes a Candle to light you to Bed
Here comes a Chopper to Chop off your Head
Chip chop chip chop - the Last Man's Dead."

This children's nursery rhyme and game, which I used to sing and play as a child, tells the sinister story of the executions of the Newgate prisoners. The "bells of Old Bailey" refer to the St. Sepulchre bell which tolled when condemned prisoners made their way from Newgate Prison towards the gallows at Tyburn or when, after 1783, they were executed outside Newgate.

On the day of their execution, convicts would dress in fine clothes, be given their last rites by the priest and then be transported, in an open ox-cart, to Tyburn – a journey of about 2.5 miles westwards away from the City. The cart was surrounded by armed officers on horseback so that no-one could attempt to rescue the prisoners along the way.

The crowd loved a "good dying" and expected to be entertained by the prisoner. If the condemned person showed any sign of fear or weakness, the crowd would express their disappointment by throwing rotten fruit and vegetables.

The first stop was at St. Sepulchre's Church, where prisoners traditionally received a nosegay of flowers. The procession then turned right down Snow Hill and left into what is now Farringdon Road and crossed the River Fleet by a narrow stone bridge. The route then took them back uphill to High Holborn. It manoeuvred through the narrow streets of St. Giles High Street, before the last part of the route along Oxford Road. The 2.5 mile journey could take up to two hours. (Reader, Holborn Viaduct hadn't been built then!)

It became a custom to stop at one or more pubs along the way so that the condemned might enjoy their last cup of ale. One such pub was the Mason's Arms, near today's Marble Arch, where only recently the manacles that held the prisoners were removed from the basement walls.

Interestingly, the phrase "on the wagon" stems from this tradition – perhaps because after the prisoners had had their last drink, they were put back on the wagon, never to drink again.

Reflection

As I sat in the graveyard of St. Sepulchre and asked my in-dwelling spirit to reveal more to me about the church's role in the Newgate prison and the executions, I began to hear the moans and cries of the prisoners. They were in hell on earth. I sensed that death seemed like a release to them, even though many of them believed they were going to hell for their crimes.

Do you remember a time when we believed in a punishing god, that violent anthropomorphic God of the Old Testament? *"And I will execute great vengeance upon them with furious rebukes; and they shall know that I am the LORD, when I shall lay my vengeance upon them."* Ezekiel 25:17.

This not-so-subtle threat suggests that no matter what kind of punishment humans could mete out to one another on earth, there was always something more sinister and final coming from the Great Judge in the sky.

I invite you to consider the possibility that God has nothing to do with the punishment we experience on earth. Perhaps all punishment comes from the superstitious notion that we have believed in and agreed upon, namely that God is a punishing God and we are wicked sinners so we deserve to be punished? And it is non-negotiable. This is a hell of its own kind - this mental and emotional prison of being doomed to punishment on earth and in the afterlife.

Actually what we have called God – referring to the cloud-enthroned autocrat of Reward and Punishment — is simply Cosmic Justice or the Law of the Universe: what goes around comes around. Or as Isaac Newton put it: "For every action there is an equal and opposite reaction." Period. Nothing to do with an angry, punishing God. We are punished by our own actions. No wonder so many were jailed and went to their death with the strong race consciousness belief that *"the wages of sin is death"* Romans 6:23. That intensity of belief in sin and punishment, supported by mass agreement, had to manifest in an inhumane legal and penal system.

As you take the walk from Newgate to Tyburn down Snow Hill, up to High Holborn, along New Oxford Street and Oxford Street ending at Marble Arch, imagine yourself in the position of the prisoners. They were jeered at and spat upon. They had rotten fruit thrown at them. This was the outer manifestation of the prisoner's own internal self-attack.

Ask yourself: how have you

- attacked yourself?
- persecuted yourself?
- shamed yourself?
- called yourself guilty?
- made yourself wrong?
- condemned yourself to death and
- not been able to release yourself from the prison of your own destructive thinking?

The evil is not in you. It never was. It was simply a mesmeric suggestion you accepted and believed to be the truth about you. You believed you were human and had a life separate and apart from God. This was your only sin and even that is only a matter of ignorance. You believed you were a sinner, that you would be punished, that death was your lot. *"...as thou hast believed, so be it done unto thee."* Matthew 8:13.

So how do we get free?

- By knowing the Truth that sets us free. "I AM the beloved of God, have never sinned, will never die."
- By cleaning up the wreckage we have created in our human ignorance and by making amends
- By practising forgiveness and compassion towards the aspect of ourselves that is undeveloped and immature, that is

selfish and short-sighted and makes mistakes. Some call this aspect of self the inner child or the dark shadow. This side of yourself needs to be embraced, understood, forgiven, and accepted by the Awakened Being that you really are.

There is no god outside you who will forgive you. Other people can forgive you, but that only really helps them. You and I are not off the hook until we have done the inner work on ourselves. You will know when the work has been done because the people who you thought were your enemies will stop throwing rotten vegetables at you. (Figuratively speaking.)

Sense of separation (sin):
evil, false judgment, accusation, attack, criticism, punishment, deprecation, character assassination, condemnation, shame, guilt

Spiritual Principles:
Innocence, Forgiveness, Mercy Compassion, Surrender

Prayer

Knowing that there is only One Power of Unconditional Love that has created everything out of Itself in the image and likeness of Absolute Perfection, I know that I am made in the perfect image of God. The One Holy Power is too pure to behold iniquity. It simply does not register it for in Its Mind there is no evil, there is no wrong doing.

I know that in Truth I am One with the Almighty. I can never be separate from God. The "I" that I AM does not know about evil or wrong doing, could not commit a crime, could not attack or hurt or condemn or shame Itself or any aspect of Itself.

I know that I am joined in Love and Truth with all beings everywhere. In Truth we are all pure and innocent, made in the image and likeness of pure holiness. I AM, and we are joined with all the prisoners who made the journey from Newgate and St. Sepulchre to Tyburn, and we are joined with every individual in the crowd who watched the procession, and, finally, we are joined with the executioners.

I AM that I AM. This is my Divine Identity. I speak this Word now, releasing myself and all beings from any seeming burden of shame, guilt, condemnation or punishment. I declare that we are born free of all sense of being tainted, evil, incorrigible or shame-based. All of the sinful conditioning of the forefathers and foremothers that we have innocently carried and erroneously believed is now being exposed in the Light of pure awareness that it might be dissolved back into its native nothingness.

The Spirit that I am has never sinned and never made a mistake. I accept that all seeming mistakes were simply an erroneous human perception.

I AM now free from the unreal realm of duality, from concepts of reward and punishment, guilty and innocent, fair and unfair, oppressor and victim, executioner and condemned. WHO I AM is simply not defined by these opposing concepts!

I stand strong and dwell now in peaceful communion with all the old warring aspects of my human self. I accept and acknowledge, love and honour all the aspects of myself that are in the learning process, the aspects of myself that are "waking up" to recognition of their true self. There is nothing in me that can judge or condemn. I am filled with love, understanding and compassion for all aspects of myself that are in the growing process and all aspects of myself that are currently showing up as my brothers and sisters on the planet.

I now release and forgive all those who I have ever thought were judging me, condemning me or persecuting me. I release them because I now know they were just reading the lines on the script that I wrote. I am free in this god-given ability to take absolute responsibility for everything that shows up in my world. I am free from condemnation because I no longer have it in me to indulge any self-condemnation. I only relate to myself with love and acceptance from this point forth. I only give compassion to myself for every action and reaction. The past is not the precedent. I am free now from all sin, shame and condemnation.

I now declare that whatever process is necessary for me to be able to live in love with myself, to forgive myself every moment and all others, is now being revealed to me and in a way that I can understand and practice. I declare that the capacity to forgive myself is established within me and that this book is simply the conduit for this knowledge to be transmitted through me to assist and uphold all beings.

I give thanks that the inner work of self-forgiveness is already done. I give thanks for the perfect process of self-forgiveness now being revealed so that it can be shared with everyone on the planet. I give thanks that the sins of the fathers and mothers have now been dissolved into their native nothingness. I give thanks that I am healed and whole, loved and adored, blessed and held in the loving arms of the Infinite Power.

I release this Word to the Law and let It be. And so It is. Amen.

Notes

Station 7
MARBLE ARCH
Alight here for
TYBURN

Marble Arch Station is on the Central Line.

Address of Site: On the traffic island in the middle of Edgeware Road at its junction with Bayswater Road.

Directions to Site: From Marble Arch Tube, pass the Marble Arch on your left. Cross to the traffic island on Edgeware Road and you will see the plaque on the ground. The site is marked by three brass triangles mounted on the pavement. The Tyburn Convent nearby is dedicated to the memory of the martyrs executed at the Tyburn Tree, and in other locations, for the Catholic faith. It is located at 8 Hyde Park Place, London W2 2LJ.

Fig. 40:   The stone plaque on the site of the Tyburn Triple Tree

"All violence is the result of people tricking themselves into believing that their pain derives from other people and that consequently those people deserve to be punished."

Marshall B. Rosenberg

History

Tyburn was a small village outside London, about 2.5 miles from Newgate prison, where criminals and innocents were hanged from 1196 until 1783. Named after the River Tyburn, which flows underground to the Thames, the "Tyburn Tree" was erected in 1571 — a wooden three-cornered structure designed for mass executions. On 23 June 1649, 24 prisoners were hanged simultaneously.

Since executions were a popular source of entertainment, as well as a money making venture, they had to take place in a large field outside the City in order to provide plenty of space for the spectators who would pay to sit on the stands. Execution days were treated as public holidays.

"Tyburn" became a euphemism for capital punishment. To "take a ride to Tyburn" (or simply "go west") was to go to one's hanging. The "Lord of the Manor of Tyburn" was the public hangman. "Dancing the Tyburn jig" was the act of being hanged.

Fig. 41: The Tyburn Hanging Tree

Not all those hanged at Tyburn had committed a capital offence – some were staunch Catholics sentenced to death because they refused to accept Henry VIII as Head of the Church. As such, they were labelled traitors.

Once the procession arrived at Tyburn from Newgate, the blindfolded and hooded prisoners, still standing on the back of the wagon, were strung up to the Triple Tree. The horses were whipped into running, leaving the prisoners to hang and die in agony by strangulation.

After the public hangings, the dead bodies were buried in the land around the Tyburn Tree – the area now known as Hyde Park and Speaker's Corner. If family members of the deceased had watched the hanging, they would try to grab the dead body as soon as possible in order to give it a proper burial according to the Christian Faith; they believed that the dead family member would not have a chance of getting to Heaven otherwise.

Another group of spectators had a vested interest in the dead bodies because they were anatomists who wanted the corpses for medical research and teaching purposes. There was money in dead bodies and sometimes it was a race between the family members and the anatomists' "assistants" to see who could claim the body first. People did not freely donate their organs then because they were afraid of not going to Heaven if they were not complete in body.

Reflection

Since the plaque is on a very busy street, I recommend taking the short walk down to the Tyburn Convent and going inside to sit in the silence and reflect on the material in this chapter. The peace in there is like a balm for the soul after the noise of the busy street.

It is uncomfortable to acknowledge how barbaric our forefathers and foremothers were. Even more uncomfortable to acknowledge how barbaric we are still capable of being, preferring to project that inner violent streak on to the world outside ourselves rather than own it as a part of our shadow.

When I first read about medieval Londoners being willing to pay to be entertained by the hangings, I was horrified. But then I realised that today we are no different: for many of us, our hungry shadow still licks its lips and is willing to pay to watch violent movies or violent news programmes or play violent games using computer software and call it all "entertainment."

What is the cause for this appetite for violence? Is it our sense of human powerlessness and our lust for power that sparks a desire to watch people violate others, while we observe from the safety of our own "spectator stands," our TVs and movie screens? I suspect that it serves our deep human desire for self-preservation – to be able to watch others being punished for their "crimes" or wounded in a war and feel the sweet relief of merely witnessing and therefore surviving.

In our reptilian brain, we are running with the protection of the pack - we do not wish to be the weak or sick victim who gets left behind and eaten by lions. No, we want to be amongst the strongest, the fittest, who survive to kill for another day's food. When we were living in caves and dressed in bear skins, perhaps that was a good thing. But now the only urban monsters we have to pit ourselves against in order to "survive" are our bosses, the traffic and maybe our biological families.

As adults, we have a choice whether or not we tune in to violent images on TV or pay to see movies with our internal violence projected on to the big screen or play computer games that feed a human desire to win by killing the enemy. Our children are not at choice, however. We should not be surprised when they start committing violent acts at a young age, join gangs, take knives to school etc. We have trained them to believe that this is acceptable behaviour – even necessary in the race for survival.

As the violence in the inner city and all over the world escalates, prisons and detention centres are inadequate to deal with the problem. Punishing people for being violent is not a deterrent.

Early conditioning is the training ground; negative patterns of behaviour instilled during gestation and in the pre-verbal years are the hardest ones to shift. As adults, we have the choice to integrate our violent shadow. We also have the choice to monitor what we expose our children to on-screen in the home.

For those whose self-preservation drive shows up as greed for income derived from violent programming and whetting the consumer appetite for more gore, may the Law of the universe be revealed to them: what goes around comes around. We cannot deliberately violate without being violated. We cannot take without being taken from. We cannot manipulate another to fulfill our own selfish agendas without being manipulated in return.

Sense of separation (sin):
fear, domination, victimhood, violence, pain, death, murder

Spiritual Principles:
Love, Life, Fulfillment

Prayer

The Power that made us out of Itself is the Power of Life, sustaining and maintaining Its own in a dimension of Peace and Harmony – the Kingdom of Heaven Consciousness. It is Life that cannot die, Life that cannot contradict or violate Its own nature, Life that is never divided against itself, Life that rejoices in Its own pure expression, Life that is evolving and revealing more of its innate Perfection with every breath that we take, Life that is whole and complete unto Itself at all points within Itself.

This Power is the Omni-active Power of Love. The Power that loves Its neighbour as Itself since in Truth there is no neighbour - there is only One of us here. The Power of Peace, Harmony and Love prevail in and through every single cell of Creation. I AM a cell of Creation.

My true nature therefore, is Peace Harmony and Love. And I know this is true for all beings everywhere, whether they have passed from view in the physical realm or whether they are waiting to appear.

As a cell in the Divine Creation, I am intimately and irrevocably connected with every other cell. Each cell of Creation is a brother or a sister. Each cell of Creation is another unique aspect of the Whole. Since we are One, it is impossible for any one of us to harm another in thought word or deed without simultaneously harming ourselves. Conversely, it is impossible for any one of us to extend peace and harmony to another without having it returned to ourselves.

I speak this Word for Peace for all those parts of my Self who were hanged at Tyburn Tree, for all those who have ever been imprisoned and put to death in London or at any site in the world at any time, past or future. I know that, in truth, no one dies. There is only Life and Life is eternal. I know that it makes no difference to the perfection of the soul whether physical organs are removed after death and used for medical research or whether they are buried in the body in the ground and rot or whether the body is burned to ashes. The Soul lives on.

I speak this Word to forever erase the notion of original sin. Every child born is a gift of sinless divine potential. I hereby dispel the notion that God is a punishing God and delivers Its punishment for sins, real or imagined, through the act of execution. The Power of Life cannot go out of integrity with itself. It cannot, therefore, kill that which It has lovingly created, maintained and sustained. I cast out of consciousness the notion that God is an external authority figure who metes out punishment through violent means as a method of teaching spiritual virtues and improving character and behaviour.

There is no one and nothing external to ourselves. The only God there is, is the God that we are now, evolving into ever greater depths and heights of awareness, experiencing the consequences of all our actions whether life-affirming or life-alienating, witnessing the out-picturing of our reptilian, conditioned mindsets as well as the ever expanding awareness of our divinity. We are our own Divine Authority. Therefore, all old tendencies to punish and harm the self, or to project this antiquated tendency on to others and make them our judges and executioners, are now neutralised. In Truth, no life can be taken and no one can take Life.

I speak this Word for the executioners, for forgiveness and for blessing, understanding that they were simply fulfilling what their culture demanded of them, embodying the courage to take the action that others did not dare to take for fear of the taint upon their soul. I speak this Word now to erase any accumulated sense of guilt and to open any hearts that were hardened in order to fulfill their task without any natural feelings of remorse or horror.

This Word of Truth sets free all executioners from guilt and it also unravels the karmic cords with those whom they were called to put to death – there is only One Life and this Life cannot be killed. Each person who was hanged at Tyburn Tree or who has been put to death had already written their part in the drama, had already chosen how they would meet their end and who would facilitate that process. No-one is guilty. Everyone is accountable.

I now speak this Word for True Power and Perfect Satisfaction for all people who have ever enjoyed or craved entertainment through violence. I declare that this old biological and psychological drive for power and self-preservation is even now being surrendered.

I declare that the evolutionary impulse to grow and develop as a Whole Being is now being quickened. The innate understanding that hurting one hurts the whole now prevails. Thus, as willing instruments for the expression of Divine Power, I decree that all beings are now moved from within to respect and care for all life forms including the planet Earth upon which we dwell. The activity of Divine Stewardship, the act of nurturing the self, others and the life forms within our local and global environment, is the very act of love which releases Infinite Power and which satiates the soul. The old tendency to consume is now dismantled in consciousness and the sacred impulse to give and to extend self in service to others is now established for all time.

Furthermore, I take my stand and declare that from this point forth, I no longer feed the addiction to violent self-destruction within my own consciousness.

I declare that all technological developments and the media of communication across the planet are now dedicated to the service of humanity, fulfilling their right and holy purpose. I speak this Word for Wisdom and Righteous Judgment around the design, the delivery and the acceptance of programming for entertainment. I declare that our computer screens and our TV screens are the holy shrines where images of our divinity are reflected to us for the greater upliftment of the Whole.

I give thanks for this Word that has been spoken, this Word of Release from guilt, this Word of forgiveness, this Word of Liberation around all false appetites, this Word for the embodiment of True Power as instruments of the Divine. I give thanks that the work has been done in consciousness and new law has been set into motion.

I release this Word into Law and allow It to be. Amen.

Notes

Station 8
BARBICAN
Alight here for
CHARTERHOUSE SQUARE

Barbican Station is on the Hammersmith & City, Metropolitan and Circle Line. *Address of Site:* Charterhouse Square, Islington EC1. www.charterhouse.org *Directions to Site:* Exit Barbican Tube Station and turn left into Aldersgate Street. Turn first left into Carthusian Street. Walk about 200 metres and you will be in Charterhouse Square with the old 14th century priory on the opposite side of the green.

Fig. 42:   Charterhouse Square – London's largest plague pit

"We cannot heal successfully while we recognize sickness as a reality to the Spirit. In spiritual healing by this method, no one believes in disease, it has no action nor reaction, it has neither cause nor effect; it has no law to support it and no one through whom it can operate."

Ernest Holmes

History

Charterhouse Square is believed to be the biggest plague pit in London where approximately 40 000 to 50 000 bodies were buried in the time of the Black Death that ravaged London from 1348 to 1350.

The Black Death began in China in 1346 and swept across Asia and Europe. It seems that the infection was carried to England by the rats, that lived on the ships bound for London, from all over the world. It wasn't actually the rats that carried the disease, but the particular type of flea that lived on their bodies. The people of medieval London were accustomed to living with rats in their homes. The streets of London were open sewers. No one suspected the rats, much less the fleas or the unhygienic conditions, as causes or carriers of the plague. They had rather more superstitious beliefs:

- God is angry with us because we are sinners
- Our wells have been poisoned
- The planets are badly aligned against us
- A witch has cursed us
- The stench of the sores corrupts the air and infects us if we breathe it in.

The children's rhyme, *"A ring, a ring o' roses, A pocket full o'posies-Atishoo atishoo, We all fall down"* has typically been associated with the plague because sufferers got a rosy rash on their skin, they carried posies of sweet-smelling herbs and flowers to protect themselves from breathing in the infected air and then they sneezed before they fell down dead.

As the plague claimed more and more lives, the graveyards in the parish churches in London became full to overflowing: corpses were being buried too close to the surface and the stench of rotting diseased flesh was repulsive. In order to provide a suitable burial site, a piece of land was leased from St. Bartholomew's priory in West Smithfield by the wealthy philanthropist, Walter de Manny. A cemetery chapel was quickly built on the site to provide

Christian burials and this land then became London's largest plague pit. In 1371 the land was granted to the Carthusian order of monks and a priory was built here called Charterhouse.

In 1611 the property was bought by Thomas Sutton and became a hospital, an alms house for single men and a school. The famous Charterhouse school has now moved to Surrey but the building is still functioning as an alms house and medical school for St. Bart's hospital nearby.

Reflection

When I arrived at Charterhouse Square, I happened to meet a resident of the alms house and I asked him if he knew anything about the plague pit. He told me that no bones have been found under the green, which is why there is some doubt as to whether it was a plague pit or not. He obviously wasn't bothered about any lingering spirits because he then opened the gate in the fence around the green with his privileged key and took the short cut along the path to his home in the priory.

Since it was getting dark by this time and raining slightly, I stood in the lighted doorway of one of the buildings overlooking the green and asked to have the truth be revealed to me regarding the plague pit. As I inwardly got still with my question and tuned in mentally to that particular period of time in our collective past, I began to get a sense of the City of London in those dark days... Deathly quiet. No one left their house if they could help it. Empty streets. There were the sounds of coughing and sneezing, some screams of pain and everywhere the smell of decaying, poisoned flesh.

Suddenly, I heard a voice within that sounded like it was coming from the depths of the grave:

"My soul cries out! Have I angered the Lord? Why such a terrible punishment? God surely does not love me. If He did, he would have saved my children and me. I was helpless. There was nothing I could do against this plague. Nothing worked. No doctors. No pomanders. No remedies. No prayers. Even burying our dead was dangerous because we had contact with the stench of the dead bodies in the pits and the foul air carried the plague germs. We had to send our loved ones to their graves without the last sacraments. There weren't enough priests to bury all the bodies. God took our loved ones from us and now they will burn in hell. God must have been angry with the priests too. They died. They had no immunity despite their life of prayer and chastity apart from the world of us sinners. We are all doomed to endless damnation."

I answered the cry: "That is not true. You were simply ignorant - not sinners!"

But I understood it from his perspective. The Law of the universe doesn't care whether you are ignorant or not. It just manifests what you deeply believe. But when painful things happen and you don't think you have done anything wrong to deserve such a "punishment," it certainly *feels* like God doesn't care.

Then I was just about to pray and leave the Square when I saw a face on the pavement. It was an image formed by the recent light rainfall that had dried out in patches on the concrete. I clearly discerned a young boy aged 10 – 14. A face and neck covered with sores. One eye completely blackened. Very thin and gaunt. Wasting away.

I heard him say to me: "Wait! I am not free yet!" I felt he

Fig. 43: The image of a face on the pavement – the ghost of a boy who died of the plague?

wanted to know the truth about the plague and about death so that he could come to peace. In the silence I said to him:

"The truth is that you were never born and you never died. The essence of you is immortal. Jesus said, 'Know ye not that ye are gods, children of the Most High?'"

Then I prayed: "I now declare that all those who transitioned from their human identity as a result of the plague are set free in this instant from all false beliefs in death and damnation. These beliefs are not real. They just acted as if they were real because so many people believed and agreed that they were true. By this Word, I dissolve now the belief in hell and the devil. They are simply human constructs. There is only one Power. It is Love. It does not punish or kill Its Own."

As humans we punish and kill ourselves by means of our erroneous thoughts, words and deeds that are the result of universal hypnotism.

The boy asked: "Could I have overridden death?"

I answered: "In Truth, yes. But given the circumstances you were in and the beliefs that prevailed then, probably not. By the time the belief in sickness and death reaches the physical level of manifestation, it is usually too entrenched to be dissolved without spiritual help. Plus the historical weight of all previous mass beliefs is too hard to fight on your own. But do not be discouraged. God is not punishing you for sin. Sin is not real. Death is not real. But Grace is real and there is Mercy.

I surrender you now into the arms of the Almighty who loves you as Its own precious son. Fly Home in peace. May your spirit be bathed in Light! I love you, little one. You are my brother."

Then I felt him smiling serenely and I walked on in peace.

Sense of separation (sin):
sickness, disease, contagion, sin, punishment, victim, helpless

Spiritual Principles:
Life, Wholeness, Grace, Well-Being.

Prayer

*There is One Power. It is Perfect Whole and Eternal Life, ever
sustaining and maintaining Itself in and as Its own Creation. Every
single cell of its Divine Body Temple is an expression of Wholeness. The
Perfect Mind / Body of God can never be sick or diseased or corrupted.*

*I know that I am One with the Mind of God. My body is the Holy
Temple of the Divine and can never be separate from the One Holy
Source of All Creation. Every action, every function, every organ,
every cell, every muscle, every fibre is formed after a holy pattern of
Perfection. Life expresses Itself radiantly through the instrument of
my body. The Divine within me has never been sick, has never
suffered and will never die.*

*I know that I am connected with all beings everywhere forwards
and backwards through time. Each one of us is a cell in the
universal body of God.*

*I speak this Word now specifically for all my brothers and sisters who
made their transition during the plague. I declare that their souls
live on for there is only One Power and that is the Power of Life.
There is nothing on earth in the visible world of effect that is
stronger than the Power of Life. There is nothing that can kill or
take this essential Life.*

*I cast out of consciousness any false or superstitious belief that God
would punish its Beloved Creation by sending a sickness to afflict
and kill. This is nonsense! I claim now that the knowledge of Truth
dissolves all superstitious beliefs back into the nothingness from
whence they came!*

*I cast out of consciousness now all beliefs in disease and contagion,
also all beliefs in a mental, emotional or physical cause for a physical
disease or contagion. The body of God is sacrosanct and cannot get*

diseased, nor can it pass on or accept an infection. As this Word is spoken, I know that the influence of universal hypnotism around disease and death is now being neutralized.

I now bless all the beings who have transitioned out of this human experience with symptoms of disease in the body. I declare that they are eternally moving on to their greater-yet-to-be with ease and grace. I know for them that their soul work in this human incarnation was done and they no longer needed a physical instrument to evolve on the plane of consciousness called Planet Earth.

With this Word of Truth, I now wipe out any past sense of agony or confusion within those who were bereaved and especially within the parents who released their children beyond the Veil. I speak this Word for Peace and Acceptance for all parents who have ever been in the position of releasing one or more children in to the Arms of the Infinite.

I declare that even now the seeming burden of grief is being lifted. Even now, the connection between parent and child remains sacrosanct. Even now, the bond of love shared between parent and child continues to unfold and deepen in its sweetness throughout all eternity. Nothing can separate those who have loved, not even the appearance of death.

I declare that all the plague burial sites in London and all around the world are now cleansed by the pure breath of Spirit. The healing power of Divine Love now flows in around and through all of the graves ushering in peace to all souls who were lost or confused and who did not know to move towards the Light of Heaven. All sense of separation from the perfect Holy Life of God is now ended. The Truth spoken has now set all beings free.

I give thanks for this Word of Truth. I give thanks for the Peace that is now established within the Charterhouse plague pit and indeed all the plague pits in and around London and the world. I give thanks that the notion of disease and contagion are now erased from consciousness. I give thanks that the Spirit of Truth is the Healer, ever revealing more of its own holy nature through and as its Divine Body Temple.

I release my Word into Law and allow It to be. Amen.

Notes

STATION 9
WESTMINSTER
Alight here for
WESTMINSTER PALACE &
THE HOUSES OF PARLIAMENT

Westminster Station is on the District and Central Line.
Address of Site: City of Westminster   www.parliament.uk
For debate information:
Tel: 020 7219 4272 House of Commons
Tel: 020 7219 3107 House of Lords
Directions to Site: Take exit 3 from Westminster Tube. Cross the
road towards Big Ben. Turn left along Parliament Square.

Fig. 44:   Palace of Westminster

"Be the change you want to see in the world"

Mahatma Gandhi

History

"Westminster" refers to the area around Westminster Abbey and the Palace of Westminster. Its name is derived from the West Minster, or monastery church, west of St. Paul's Cathedral in the City of London. The area has been the seat of the government of England for almost a thousand years.

"The Westminster System" is the name given to the parliamentary model of democratic government that has evolved in Britain. It has been adopted as a foundation for governments in many other nations, particularly in the British Commonwealth and other parts of the former British Empire.

The Houses of Parliament occupy the medieval Palace of Westminster. The Palace was first built by King Canute in ca 1020 and used by William the Conqueror as his London base from 1066 onwards. At the end of the 11th century, William's successor,

Fig. 45: Big Ben

William Rufus, transformed it into an edifice of great beauty for the royalty and nobility of his day.

Until an outbreak of fire in 1512, during the reign of King Henry VIII, several monarchs had made the palace their London base. Henry decided to move the court to Whitehall Palace. From this time on, Westminster Palace functioned as the seat of government. The Royal Courts of Justice were also housed in this building but are now located in the Strand.

Westminster Hall

Westminster Hall is the main survivor of the medieval Palace of Westminster, escaping the 1834 fire that burned down every other building in the vicinity, and is now the vestibule of the House of Commons.

Besides hosting the first meeting of Parliament in 1265, Edward II was also deposed here in his absence. Sir Thomas More was tried for treason in 1535 and condemned to death. The Catholic King Charles I was tried here in January 1649 and publicly beheaded three days later outside Banqueting House.

Westminster Hall is now mainly used for ceremonial events. South Africa's former political prisoner and opponent of Apartheid, President Nelson Mandela, came to address both the House of Lords and the House of Commons from the steps of Westminster Hall in 1996. There is also a statue of him outside in Parliament Square. Clearly who is "in" and who is "out" is simply a matter of time and opinion. Fortunately for those who are currently "out", there have not been many beheadings lately...

Fig. 46: Westminster Hall in the Palace of Westminster, London, 1808.

House of Lords Crypt

The **Gunpowder Plot** was a failed attempt by a Catholic group to assassinate the Protestant King James I of England and VI of Scotland. It was feared that he would increase the persecution of Catholics that had been initiated by Henry VIII when he broke away from the Pope and declared himself Head of the Church of England.

At midnight on Wednesday, 5 November 1605, Guy Fawkes was discovered in the crypt under the House of Lords guarding twenty plus barrels of gunpowder, preparing to blow up Parliament and King James. Fawkes was arrested and tortured before being executed.

Fig. 47: Guy Fawkes by artist George Cruikshank (1792-1878), 1840.

Eventually, eight men in the group were caught and sentenced to death in January 1606. To this day, Yeomen of the Guard search the Lords' cellars before the State Opening of Parliament. Unfortunately, this area is closed to the general public.

The thwarting of the Gunpowder Plot has led to our quaint British custom of making and then burning a "guy" (a life-sized dummy of a man) on bonfires in our back gardens on November 5 each year and letting off fireworks while we munch on hot sausage rolls and cups of tea (or alcoholic beverages) to keep from freezing in the cold damp winter air.

Reflection

We mostly live in an "either/or, right/wrong, dominate/avoid domination, fight/flee, in-group/out-group" world until we develop sufficiently internally to see the world through the eyes and heart of: "both-and, win-win, love the perceived enemies and all life is sacred." I believe that we are all headed in this direction; it is the gift and mandate of our evolutionary journey. We can support it or thwart it with our free will.

Everyone has their own concept of good self-preservation for themselves and maybe even for the world. We can spend our energy fighting for the superior rightness of our concepts or we can surrender to that Energy, which some choose to call God, who governs the universe perfectly as One Whole and Holy system.

I remember being a classic victim, an armchair socialist, although I did not have an armchair to my name since I lived in a humble squat in Amsterdam in my early twenties when my political rage was at its most vehement. I was a socialist feminist. The male politicians, I thought, were an elite bunch of privileged toffs, dedicated to passing the laws that would blatantly (in the case of the Conservative Party) or covertly (in the case of the Labour Party) ensure that the rich got richer and the poor got poorer.

Enjoying a lofty view from my 2nd floor squat in downtown Amsterdam, I firmly believed that the cause of peace, in Britain and the world, could only be significantly furthered by a large number of well-appointed castrations!

At that time, I did not appreciate that growing up in Britain meant I was entitled to a wealth of privileges that most of the citizens on our planet will never experience in their lifetime: enough food, clean water, education, free health and dental care, and opportunities to work or to claim unemployment benefits. It took me a while to realise I was simply rebelling against my own internalized concepts of authority that I projected out on to politicians: they had the power and I didn't, but I should have and therefore I was angry!

In an effort to heal myself of 30 years of "contempt prior to investigation," while researching for this book, I attended two debates in Parliament, one in the House of Commons on Food Poverty and another in the House of Lords on Capping Welfare Benefits.

I heard wonderful women speakers in the House of Commons – one of them looked like she was in her early thirties – who were clearly up to bat for the community that had elected them and doing their best to create a greater good for the whole. In the House of Lords, I noticed deep compassion and caring in the tone and content of the Lords' speeches – a genuine desire to do the right thing for the majority.

If you go to a debate, assume that whatever motion is up for discussion is exactly what you are meant to pray for. Rather than praying for the team to win whose point of view you support, speak your Word silently for Divine Government to reveal Itself, for the politicians to be guided by their inner integrity, their vision for the future, their wisdom and their compassion for the people of Britain and others in the world whose lives are changed by decisions that are made in these hallowed halls.

Politicians are not gods regardless of how they might view themselves. We vote for them consciously or unconsciously. They represent the mass consciousness of the people. Members of Parliament are in power by right of consciousness - they expect it and accept it. When they no longer represent the consciousness of the people, they are voted out of office or get exposed for corruption or retire or move on. Some have been murdered or beheaded. There is no point in criticising them or pretending that we are victims of the current government because we have silently elected our own body of oppressors in all phases of our lives by putting the responsibility for our well being onto others.

This insidious pattern of projection will always backfire. It is not wise to be children in matters of state and to expect politicians to be our co-dependent parents who give us everything we want. Looking to outer authorities to create positive change in our lives keeps us stuck in a state of powerlessness. It is for us to acknowledge our own inner power to self-govern and to create the world of experience that we would wish to inhabit.

My first spiritual teacher in South Africa, Rev. Gladys Harrison, said: "When you read the newspapers and hear yourself saying, 'Why don't they...?' it is a heavenly clue about your purpose on earth."

Sense of Separation (sin):
false power, false prophets, misguidance, abuse, exploitation, anger, rebellion, projection.

Spiritual Principles:
True Power, Peace, Wisdom, Divine Government, Inner Authority, Divine Stewardship

Prayer

There is One Whole Power. It is the Omnipresence, Omnipotence and Omniscience that governs every single cell of Its beloved Creation now and forever. This is the Power that governs my life. It governs the life of everyone reading this prayer right now. It governs the life of every soul since we are all connected in consciousness.

I speak this Word now, with the authority vested in me as an emanation of the Most High, decreeing that the Spirit of Wisdom, Guidance and Compassion now governs the life of all beings who are involved in government. I call forth the manifest evidence of Spirit at work in all aspects of leadership and law-making and social concern.

I know that all politicians have been divinely appointed to their positions and I declare that each one is now filled with an awareness of, and a commitment to, that sacred responsibility. There are no mistakes.

The Truth is emerging even now as this Word is spoken. Any seeming lies or corruption, false ambitions, selfish manipulations, drives toward megalomania, political intrigues, financial dishonesty or abuse of position are being exposed in the light of conscious awareness. That which is not based on Truth cannot stand for it cannot sustain itself.

I bless all beings who have experienced suffering or execution as a

result of being on the wrong side of the prevailing "in-group." I
know that they were fighting for what they believed was good and
right and true based on their conditioning, decisions and experience
– exactly the same as the "in-group." There is no otherness here.
There is only One. Since there is no death in Spirit, I know that
their essence lives on.

That Divine impulse to stand for Truth and Justice and Freedom
permeates the walls of the Palace of Westminster impacting all beings
called to be there in leadership and right governance.

I speak this Word declaring forgiveness and compassion for myself
and all those who have sought their good in positions of power
through various selfish means: the crushing of an opponent or the
stealing of resources for personal consumption, the keeping of secrets
to avoid humiliating exposure of self or others.

Adolf Hitler is forgiven.

Bin Laden is forgiven.

The Ayatollah Khomeini is forgiven.

All kings, queens, dictators, politicians past present and future are
forgiven. The Spirit within me cannot behold iniquity. My Spirit
remains untouched by the sins of ignorance. This Grace and Mercy I now
accept for myself and for all who have led themselves into temptation and
simply not had enough developed spiritual muscle to change course.

With this power of Divine Authority, I declare that a new Power of
Wisdom is being ushered in – the true democracy of the Spirit,
where every life is valuable because it is the life of God made
manifest, where every person is a spiritual brother or spiritual sister,
where laws are made which support the full expression of life.
I accept now, for humankind, a quantum leap in our internal

development. The old addiction to self-preservation is now returned to its native nothingness. The passion to create, to serve, to give and to share, to govern with grace and wisdom is now being quickened in the hearts and minds of all beings everywhere.

I declare that all seeming opposing aspects of Self are welcomed home – the victim and the oppressor, the criminal and the saint, the attacker and the defender, the In-Law and the Out-Law. All false and ignorant projections are now withdrawn. They have no power to dominate our thinking. Full responsibility for the creation of our worlds is established within, now and forever.

I give thanks now for this Word that has been spoken, for the revelation of Divine Government throughout Parliament and all governments everywhere. I give thanks for Divine Authority and Responsibility being grounded in each individual soul. I give thanks for Wisdom and Truth in the governing of mind, body and body of affairs of all beings everywhere and throughout all generations.

I release this Word into Law and I allow It to be. And so It is. Amen.

Notes

Station 10
KING'S CROSS
Alight here for
BOUDICCA'S GRAVE

King's Cross Station is on the Piccadilly, Northern (Bank Branch), Circle, Metropolitan, Hammersmith & City and Victoria Line.

Address of Site: King's Cross station, Platforms 8, 9, 10 and 13 (exact location unknown).

Directions to Site: Follow directions from King's Cross Underground Station.

Fig. 48:   King's Cross Station, Platform 8

"I have cherished the ideal of a democratic and free society in which all persons live together in harmony and with equal opportunities. It is an ideal which I hope to live for and to achieve. But if needs be, it is an ideal for which I am prepared to die."

Nelson Mandela

History

There is a urban myth that the Celtic Queen, Boudicca of the Iceni tribe, was buried under the present day King's Cross Station after she died leading a rebellion against the Roman Empire in 60 CE. It is thought that this famous battle between the indigenous Celts and the Roman invaders was fought right here on the site of King's Cross Station because previously there was a small village here known as Battle Bridge. Some sources say Boudicca can be found under platform 8 or 13, others say 9 or 10.

The Iceni people were a Celtic tribe who occupied the area of Britain now known as Norfolk and North West Suffolk. The Romans invaded Britain in 43 CE. In 47 CE Prasutagus, Boudicca's husband, was recognised as King of the Iceni by the Romans and his people were not completely subjugated to Roman rule.

When King Prasutagus died in 60 CE, the Romans did not honour their previous agreement with the Iceni tribe and set out to establish total Roman control by pillaging the area. The King's widow, Queen Boudicca, complained. The Romans' reaction was to flog Queen Boudicca and force her to watch her two daughters being raped.

Boudicca then led a rebellion against the Romans, starting by laying waste Camulodunum (Colchester) and killing every Roman inhabitant. She then attacked Verulamium (St. Albans) and moved towards London. By the time Boudicca reached the northern outskirts of London, the Romans had amassed an army and the Iceni tribe were beaten with thousands of lives lost, never to rebel again. This was, however, the most severe attack on the Romans during their nearly 400-year long occupation of Britain.

You can see an impressive statue of Boudicca in her chariot with her two daughters beside her at Westminster Pier, facing Big Ben and the Houses of Parliament. She is viewed as a heroine of national resistance and the feminist cause.

Fig. 49: Statue of Queen Boudicca in her chariot with her two daughters

King's Cross has not only been the stage for the war between the Celts and the Romans, but also for more recent conflict between the IRA and the English and also between Al Qaeda and the British.

IRA Bomb 1973 at King's Cross Station

On September 10, 1973 the IRA (Irish Republican Army) set off bombs at London's King's Cross and also Euston station injuring 21 people. Why? Perhaps because of the long history of the English invading and occupying Irish land?

- In 1169 the Norman armies that had invaded Britain also invaded Ireland and managed to occupy the far eastern side of the country.
- Protestant Oliver Cromwell, having won the English Civil War against the Catholics, invaded Ireland in 1649 and gave out parcels of Irish land to his soldiers as a way of paying their salaries.

Down, Dirty and Divine

- In 1801 the British attempted to solve the "Irish Problem" by creating the Kingdom of Great Britain & Ireland. (That went down like a bomb...)

The IRA was founded in 1913 with the intention for Ireland to be free of British rule and self-governing.

Since 1994 the Peace Process has been in place between the British government and the Sinn Fein (IRA) and the weapons of war have been put down in favour of dialogue.

Al Qaeda Bombs 7/7/2005 at King's Cross Station

On 7 July, 2005, (often referred to as 7/7) during the morning rush hour, four suicide bombers were filmed entering King's Cross Station on CCTV camera at about 8:30 am. Three bombs went off on the underground within the next few minutes. Later, another bomb went off in a bus on Tavistock Square. They were detonated by Muslim suicide bombers working on behalf of Al Qaeda.

In total 52 people were killed, including the four bombers, and over 700 people were injured with extensive damage to the trains and the underground tunnels. Why did they attack? Perhaps as a result of British troops being sent to Afghanistan and Iraq to "fight the war against terrorism"?

The following is a quote from an Al Jazeera broadcast on 1 September 2005 by an Al Qaeda member:

"I and thousands like me are forsaking everything for what we believe. Our drive and motivation doesn't come from tangible commodities that this world has to offer. Our religion is Islam, obedience to the one true God and following the footsteps of the final prophet messenger. Your democratically-elected governments continuously perpetuate atrocities against my people all over the world.

*And your support of them makes you directly responsible,
just as I am directly responsible for protecting and
avenging my Muslim brothers and sisters. Until we feel
security you will be our targets and until you stop the
bombing, gassing, imprisonment and torture of my
people we will not stop this fight. We are at war and
I am a soldier. Now you too will taste the reality of
this situation."*

Reflection

The British people have had atrocities committed against them. And around the world, many nations have suffered atrocities at the hands of the British. True peace will never be achieved by violent means. When the word "peace" is bandied about in the media, it tends to mean "peace on my terms" i.e. "domination" or "the absence of war," which are very limited interpretations.

Any war or conflict is based on a false notion of limited resources - for example: money, oil, land or love. In the human game of self-preservation, the goal is to consistently get as many resources as possible and then figure out how to use and enjoy them while also stockpiling them and stopping others from taking them away.

When survival of the human identity is paramount and it seems that the "enemy" has to be eradicated in order to guarantee this survival, the seven deadly sins are in full sway: anger, jealousy, lust, greed, gluttony, avarice and envy. These can take the form of lying, cheating, stealing, raping, pillaging, desecrating, betraying, fighting or killing – whether at gross or subtle levels. Being right is everything and being wrong means death in the mind of the mad ego.

In "The Life of Mahatma Gandhi," author Louis Fischer explains the concept of non-violence: *"Satyagraha is peaceful. If words fail to convince the adversary perhaps purity, humility, and honesty will. The opponent must be 'weaned from error by patience*

and sympathy,' weaned, not crushed; converted, not annihilated…
Satyagraha is the exact opposite of the policy of an-eye-for-an-eye-for-
an-eye-for-an-eye which ends in making everybody blind… You
cannot inject new ideas into a man's head by chopping it off; neither
will you infuse a new spirit into his heart by piercing it with a dagger."

I admire anyone who is willing to die for a noble cause. To lay down one's life, that others might live in greater freedom, justice or equality, is truly an extraordinary act of selfless courage. Even though I have always had causes, I have never had the courage to die for any of them and I am humbly grateful for those who have gone ahead of me/us and, with their own lives, laid the path for the freedoms we enjoy today.

The important issue is the motivation for our wars: are they to give life or to take life? But, since you are reading this book, it is likely that you already know that there is no war to be fought "out there", that you are not the victim of external forces, nor are you the oppressor. The only righteous holy war is within our own consciousness. Despite all the evidence to the contrary, our work is to behold all beings as our brothers and sisters, to love our enemies, even when the egoic kneejerk reaction is to demonise them and fight or flee.

When he was assassinated, Ghandi chanted the name of God, blessing his killer. The followers of Martin Luther King Jr. died beholding the Divine in the white policemen who were brutalizing them. When Jesus Christ was on the cross, he prayed, "Forgive them Father, for they know not what they do." This elevated consciousness of true peace is worthy of our aspiration.

Sense of separation (sin):
fear, attack, defense, betrayal, invasion, abuse, rape

Spiritual Principles:
Peace, Love, Forgiveness, Compassion, Harmony, Abundance for all

Prayer

I know there is One Power. It is Omnipotent. It is Harmony, Peace and Unconditional Love. It functions through me, and everyone who is in any way connected to my consciousness. It is the one and only True Power that governs sustains and maintains this universe. It cannot compromise Itself, hurt or attack or defend any aspect of Itself for everything is One. There is no other power, no separate power, no enemy power, no devil.

I speak this Word now for the awareness of the One Power functioning through and as me, that harmonises everything within itself. I am one with all peoples everywhere, regardless of nation, colour or creed. I cast out of consciousness the notion of terrorism knowing that God would not terrorize itself nor would God take sides with invaders or the invaded. I speak this Word now neutralising all the human causes and, thereby, the effects of war, knowing that in the mind of God, war has never even happened.

I bless Boudicca and her daughters knowing that their souls have never been violated, their essential Self has never been invaded, occupied, raped or even killed. The eternal spirit of Boudicca is alive and well, so too all her Iceni people and all the Roman armies, so too the eternal Spirit of the four suicide bombers at King's Cross and the IRA members and all those who were either killed or wounded by the bombs.

As of now, as of this moment when this Word is spoken, I set new cause into motion. I declare that Omnipotence upholds sustains and maintains all beings everywhere in an atmosphere of community and peace. There is nothing to fight for, no-one to fight against. All false beliefs about limited resources are now dissolved by the power of this Word. I call forth the awareness of Perfect Sufficiency and All Needs Met.

I give thanks that the concept of "war against" is now eradicated in my consciousness and therefore at all points in consciousness simultaneously. I give thanks that Omnipotent Peace now reigns forever, supreme in the minds and hearts of all beings.

I release this Word into Law and I allow It to be. Amen.

Notes

Station 11
TOWER HILL
Alight here for the
TOWER OF LONDON

Tower Hill Station is on the Circle and District Line.

Address of Site: The White Tower, Tower of London.

Directions to Site: Follow signs to Tower of London from station exit.

Fig. 50: The Tower of London showing the White Tower in the centre with its four distinctive turrets

"But I say unto you, Love your enemies, bless them that curse you, do good to them that hate you, and pray for them which despitefully use you, and persecute you."

Matthew 5:44

History

Tower Hill was once a sacred site known as Bryn Gwyn where the Druids would carry out their sacred ceremonies at the times of the Equinox and the Solstice. The Druids were the spiritual leaders of the Celtic people who arrived in Britain in about 450 BCE from Central Europe. With the Roman occupation, starting in 43 CE, they gradually retreated west to Ireland and Wales, and north up to Scotland. Their sacred hill, where the Tube station is now, was later used for the executions of the Tower prisoners.

The White Tower, which is the oldest part of the collection of buildings known as the Tower of London, was built between 1078 and 1097. It was the fortress of the Norman-French King, William the Conqueror, and his display of strength over the Angles and Saxons, whose country he had invaded and occupied in 1066. It was also an important defense of his new realm, being situated at the eastern edge of the old City of London, and a deterrent to would-be invaders trying to enter London from the Thames.

The White Tower, as it is now known, got its name when the stone fortress was whitewashed in 1240.

Records show that there had been a Jewish community in London since the arrival of William the Conqueror. He had invited them from France believing that their commercial expertise would serve the growth of his new realm. Jews were permitted to function as moneylenders because, in the Catholic faith, Christians were forbidden from charging interest to fellow Christians. Lending money for interest was known as the "sin of usury." Subsequently, the Jews became very wealthy and were, at the same time, despised by the Kings and nobles who often incurred the greatest debts.

Judaism was mostly practised in private to avoid persecution. Christians held the Jews responsible for murdering Jesus and so they were regularly mobbed and tortured and even accused of murdering small Christian children in order to use the blood in their Jewish rituals. Furthermore, there were regular attacks on Jews by the Christian crusaders – in their communities throughout Europe as well as in the Holy Land.

In November 1278, when the Jewish population of London was only ca 1000, most living in the ghetto of Old Jewry, close to the Tower of London, approximately 600 Jews, mostly financiers and goldsmiths, were imprisoned for 140 days in the Tower. Some sources say they were in the sub-crypt of the White Tower that is no longer open for public viewing. Other named locations for detention mentioned in Marcus Robert's "National Anglo Jewish Heritage Trail. Fact Sheet on 'Jews and the Tower of London – a Hidden History'" include, *'in the elephant house', 'in the tower beyond the elephant', 'in Hagin's Tower', 'in Brother John's Tower', 'in Brother John's stable', and 'in Brother John's cellar.'*

The Jews had been accused of coin-clipping.

Fig. 51:   The White Tower (showing wooden staircase to first floor entrance)

Down, Dirty and Divine

The English coinage had been re-minted in 1248, but was becoming worn and damaged from years of deliberate coin-clipping, which is the process of shaving metal from the circumference of the coin and then melting it down to forge new coins. Although it is not known how many of the prisoners, if any, were actually guilty of this crime, 269 Jews were later executed at the Tower.

King Edward expelled all the Jews from England in 1290 upon the accusation of usury and disloyalty to the Crown. This automatically cancelled the King's huge debt to the Jews and also enabled him to claim all property and possessions they left behind. It was to be another 365 years before the Jews were formally allowed to move back to England in 1655.

Reflection

On anti-Semitism and religious persecution

Anti-Semitism has been described as, primarily, hatred against Jews as a race while anti-Judaism is described as hostility to the Jewish religion. In Western Christianity, anti-Judaism effectively merged into anti-Semitism during the 12th century according to Richard Harries in his book "After the evil: Christianity and Judaism in the shadow of the Holocaust."

What is it within the human psyche that judges and persecutes, often in the name of God? When all religions agree that God is a God of Love, it is curious to note how members of one religious group can justify killing those who are born into and / or practice a different religious belief?

It does not matter what we believe theoretically, what our culture believes, what our sacred texts teach, even what we espouse, if we are unconscious of ourselves as divine beings. If there is no awareness of our oneness with the Whole, then we are living in a state of separation from others. The law of self-preservation prevails - the law of being right unto death. So the persecution of any out-group by any in-group is simply a matter of claiming rightness by proving wrongness and maintaining rightness by exterminating wrongness.

This superior rightness is a form of insanity, but Hitler was not dismissed as insane while he sent Jews to their death. Admittedly, support for his views and his plan to exterminate Jews wasn't always whole-hearted or genuine: detractors would have been shot. Nevertheless, the vision of the Aryan supremacy of the 3rd Reich (Super-Self-Preservation) and its violent strategies of war and concentration camps, appealed to enough Germans to gain mass support for over 10 years – from 1933 until Hitler's suicide in 1945.

The refreshingly "unorthodox" Catholic priest, Hans Küng, in his book "On Being a Christian" points out that, *"Nazi anti-Judaism was the work of godless, anti-Christian criminals. But it would not have been possible without the almost two thousand years' pre-history of 'Christian' anti-Judaism..."*

On the victim and the oppressor cycle

While I was visiting Israel in 2004, I happened to be in Jerusalem on Jerusalem Day – the day when the Jews celebrate the reunification of Jerusalem under Israeli control. The Six-Day War of 1967 established Jewish control of the city for the first time since the destruction of the second Holy Temple by the Romans in 70 CE.

While there, I witnessed thousands of Jews marching through the streets of Jerusalem with their blue and white settler clothing, waving their banners and their flags with the Star of David. Security was tight. Palestinians were not allowed into the inner city to work on that day. It was a display of victory and supremacy which reminded me, tragically, of the World War II newsreels showing Nazi troops marching with passion and purpose, convinced that they were justified in killing the enemy in the accomplishment of their vision.

Meanwhile, the Jews have built walls dividing the West Bank (the Palestinian area west of the Jordan River which includes

Down, Dirty and Divine

Bethany, Bethlehem, Hebron and Jericho) from the Jewish areas in and around the city of Jerusalem. The walls are designed to keep the Palestinians imprisoned and intimidated. The entry points into the Jewish sections of the city are heavily guarded by young Jewish soldiers, bearing loaded machine guns, who check the ID documents of all who are passing back and forth, entitled to detain or prohibit those whom they suspect of any anti-Israeli motives.

In a state of imagined separation from God, an oppressor cannot exist without a victim. And, because what goes around comes around, according to the Universal Law of Cause and Effect, those who have been the oppressors are bound to eventually play the role of the victim and vice versa. Our human history is dotted with similar stories:

- The Romans persecuted the Christians in Rome after the crucifixion of Jesus and fed them to the lions. Then when Christianity was adopted as the official religion of the Roman Empire by Emperor Constantine in 380 CE, his successor, Emperor Theodosius, began persecuting all non-Christians, forcing them to give up their "pagan" practices on pain of death.
- In 597, Christianity became the official religion of England – the "pagan" Angles, Saxons, Celts and worshippers of the Norse gods were marginalized and persecuted by the Catholics.
- In 1538, Henry VIII desecrated the Catholic Monasteries in England, taking all the land and the treasure for the Crown, insisting that he was now Head of the Church of England, and that his subjects had to denounce the Catholic Faith and adopt the new Anglican version of Christianity. Citizens who resisted were accused of treason and executed or hanged.

The persecution of the Jews throughout Christian history, specifically in the World War II camps, and more currently, the persecution of the Palestinians by the Jews, is all simply a portrayal of the capacities that are in all of us to alternate between the role of oppressor and sacrificial victim. If we don't accept our innate tendencies to seize all human power over others and kill in order to maintain rightness or to give away all power to other humans and die to maintain rightness as victims, then we are part of an ongoing suppression of our individual and collective shadow which must result in more atrocities being reflected in the world outside us.

Will you help me to liberate humanity from this 2000-year-old wound which has been festering between Jews and Christians?

On behalf of all Christian people willing to join with me, I now release the Jews from any debt of shame or blame for their part in the crucifixion of Jesus the Christ. I thank the Jews for their karmic willingness to play the role of the "murderer" on the cosmic stage. I understand that Judas' so called "betrayal" and the Sanhedrin's agreement with the crucifixion was simply a part of the Messianic Imperative: Jesus had to go through the appearance of dying on the cross in order to fulfill his sacred mission and prove that there is no death – this to set humanity free from its egoic fear of dying. The Jews played their part perfectly – as did everyone else. It had to be the way it was.

Sense of separation (sin):
persecution, domination, victimhood, rightness, wrongness

Spiritual Principles:
Oneness, Tolerance, Acceptance, Understanding, Unity in Diversity, Love

Prayer

There is only One God, an Omnipotent, Omnipresent, Omniscient, Omniactive Power of which I am created, of which all beings are

*created. This One Power is birthless and deathless, It is infinite and
eternal and, thus, so am I and so are all beings everywhere. It unifies
everyone and everything within Itself, pouring Itself equally into
every single individual cell of its beloved Creation.*

*In this Infinite Power that is Love, I am united with all beings regardless
of race or religion, creed or tradition, beliefs or faith. No person place or
thing can separate me from my essential divinity, my salient connection
with the Divine, my intrinsic connection with all life forms past, present
and future and all unfolding in this Eternal Now.*

*I speak my Word for all religious groups who have ever had the
experience of religious persecution declaring that their essential
connection with the Divine has never been and could never be
threatened or ousted. I know that not even the phenomenon of death
could take away that Holy Selfhood which is infinite and immortal
and I accept for and about these beings that their life is sacred,
untouched, and lives on beyond their human graves.*

*I speak my Word for all individuals or religious groups who have, in
ignorance, persecuted anyone for a differing religious belief or
practice, declaring that all there is in the Mind of the Divine is
Love: Forgiveness, Understanding, Mercy and Compassion for every
emanation of Itself. Indeed, in the Mind of the Divine, persecution
and murder never happened.*

*The One Power of Absolute Love would not attack or persecute
Itself, would not take sides. It cannot. There is only One. The One
cannot know two-ness, other-ness, opposition, conflict or separation.
It can only know the many-faceted, infinite aspects of Itself. Within
the One, there is the right and the reason and the room for every
individual expression of religious belief, for every individual
connection with the Source of Being, every cultural ritual and every
mystical form of worship.*

So I now cast out of consciousness any and all concepts that may have trapped any of us in a religious/cultural identity which had us believe that we were better than, or separate from, any other religious group. I declare that all of these attachments to our former, cherished and ego-bound concepts of God are now dissolved in the light of pure awareness.

I give thanks that this Word of Truth is now established as Law in the Universe, I give thanks for the eternal forgiveness of ignorance, I give thanks for the merciful embrace of all of the unconscious aspects of humanhood, both victim and oppressor.

I give thanks that this Word acts as a laser beam of light and shines in the darkness of ignorant human beliefs and behaviours. It dissolves all sense of separation and the Beloved Community is revealed in its sacred tapestry of Prayer and Prophecy, Worship and Wisdom, Dance and Devotion, Chanting and Charity, Song and Surrender.

I release this Word to the Law and name It done. It is good, good and very good. And so I let It be. And so It is. Amen.

Notes

Station 12
TEMPLE
Alight here for
TEMPLE CHURCH

Temple Station is on the District and Circle Line.

Address of Site: Temple Place, City of London, EC4Y 7HL

www.templechurch.com   Tel: 020 7353 8559

Directions to Site: Go right out of Temple Station towards the Thames. Turn left and walk along Embankment. At the sign for Temple Church, turn left and go through the black gates with the golden lamb emblem. Then you will be in Temple Gardens. Keep walking straight ahead until you come to Pump Court Cloisters. Turn right under the arch to Temple Church.

Fig. 52:   The Temple Church showing the rounded form reminiscent of the Church of the Holy Sepulchre in Jerusalem

"We may know who we are or we may not. We may be Muslims, Jews or Christians but until our hearts become the mould for every heart we will see only our differences."

Rumi

"The conversion to Christ need not entail a conversion to the Christian religion. The word is a symbol for the Child of God within us, our true identity and a space of remembrance of all that is divine. To be His disciple is to take on the mantle of His ministry by refusing to acknowledge the ultimate reality of any walls that divide us."

Marianne Williamson

History

In 1096-1099, 1145 and 1190-93, three major crusades took place from Europe to the Holy Land. Their purpose was to regain control of Jerusalem after the Muslims had captured the city in 1076, and allow Christians access to the holy sites.

The incentive for the pilgrims to go on these crusades was that the Pope had told them that their sins would all be forgiven if they were killed defending Jerusalem from the "Infidel." The "Infidel" referred to unbelievers or people who did not believe in a particular religion but generally meant non-Christian i.e. Muslim or Jewish in the context of the Crusades.

Later, Christians were told that murdering a "Saracen" (a medieval term for Arab with its understood meaning of "enemy of Christ") would likewise earn them absolution and a place in Heaven. Some crusaders were motivated by greed and the promise of rich treasures from the East. Others simply wanted a legal way to avoid paying taxes!

The Knights Templar was founded as a monastic-military order in Jerusalem in the year 1118 after the First Crusade. The knights were identifiable by the white shift covering their armour with the red cross on the front. Their original purpose was to protect pilgrims on the crusades. It was understood that their duty was to kill for Christ. Sean Martin, on page 35 of his book "The Knights Templar: The History and Myths of the Legendary Military Order" explains that this was acceptable, even honourable, because Bernard of Clairvaux – one of the most respected churchmen of the day – condoned it in his treatise "In Praise of the New Knighthood" in which he made the distinction between *homicide* that was a sin and *malecide* that was not a sin because it meant "the killing of evil."

The Knights Templar were originally known as "The Order of the Poor Knights of the Temple of Solomon": "poor" because they donated all their wealth to the organization when they took their vows and "Temple of Solomon," because they were headquartered in Jerusalem in the Al-Aqsa Mosque on the Temple Mount for most of the twelfth century until 1187 when Saladin's forces captured Jerusalem.

Unsolved mysteries surround the Templars as to their true activities during the 68 years on Temple Mount. Some believe they were searching for, and possibly even in possession of, secret treasure: precious stones from the foundations of the second Jewish Temple, the relics of saints, pieces of the True Cross upon which Jesus was crucified, the embalmed head of St. John the Baptist, the Ark of the Covenant, and perhaps one of these treasures was even the Holy Grail – the blood of Christ contained in the sacred chalice.

The Temple Church in London was built in 1185 as part of a large monastic complex that includes the Inner Temple and Middle Temple. It served as the Templars' headquarters in Britain and as a training establishment for the knights where strict religious and military discipline was imposed.

As London's earliest Gothic church, it has an unusual design with its circular nave replicating the sacred geometry of the Church of the Holy Sepulchre in Jerusalem. It was in this circular nave of the London Temple Church where initiate monks would go through their initiation ceremonies and take their vows of piety, chastity, poverty and obedience. The actual content of the ceremony has always been a well-kept secret.

In 1307 the Templar order was destroyed and abolished. The Templars were accused of heresy and, in 1310, 54 Templars were burned at the stake. King Edward II of England took control of the Temple church but later gave it to the Knights Hospitaller (a similar order of monks whose mission was to care for the sick pilgrims in the Holy Land).

The Hospitaller Knights rented the Inner Temple and the Middle Temple to two colleges of lawyers. They constitute two of the four Inns of Court – the other two being Gray's Inn and Lincoln's Inn.

Miraculously, the Great Fire of London in 1666 only came as far as the Master's House on the east side of the Temple and did not touch the church itself. In 1678, the next fire stopped right before the west entrance and did not touch the consecrated ground around the church.

What is so distinctive and unusual about this church are the ten stone tombs of the knights arranged on the floor of the round church. Nine are effigy tombs and one has no effigy but only a sarcophagus lid. They were believed to be tombs until the post-WWII restoration revealed no bodies, but only effigy memorials. Perhaps you recall the scene in the movie of Dan Brown's bestselling book "The Da Vinci Code"? Which one do you find yourself being drawn to?

Reflection

On the Crusades

I sat by the tomb without an effigy knight. The plaque says "Attribution Unknown." As I tuned into the spirit of this knight (who may or may not have been buried here) within my own consciousness, this is what passed between us.

SC: Talk to me, Knight, from your stony grave. Tell me about the Crusades.

Knight: We were fighting for a holy cause. This justified killing and warfare.

SC: What was your holy cause?

Fig. 53:   Tomb of the unidentified Knight Templar in the Temple Church

Knight: Establishing the Christian Faith in the Holy City of Jerusalem. To do that we had to remove the Infidels. We wanted to establish a Christian stronghold in Jerusalem that could never be attacked nor undermined. I felt like Christ's divinely appointed emissary on earth. I gave everything for the cause. I gave it willingly.

SC: Thank you, Knight. I can feel your religious zeal. It reminds me of the zeal I witness today in the Holy Land, between the Palestinian Arabs and the Jews – both groups are willing to kill for what they believe to be a holy cause. Yet the Master told us that if we live by the sword, we will have to die by the sword. If I take life, no matter how justified I think I am, my life will be taken for this is the karmic law.

Knight: I understand that now, but then we were caught up in a passionate frenzy and we truly believed we were doing God's will. We had to protect the Holy City. It was the symbol of the Kingdom of Heaven on

Earth. Our own death meant nothing to us in the battle for righteousness.

SC: Rest in peace, Knight. 700 years after your order was destroyed, the Church of the Holy Sepulchre in Jerusalem is thriving and Christian pilgrims can visit from all over the world. Your mission was accomplished although, perhaps, not in the way you imagined. I will pray for you and your brother Templars and all crusaders and all who have ever murdered or been murdered in the name of God. May your soul find solace.

On the possibility of peace in the Holy Land: the Sulha and Arab-Israeli conflict resolution

In August 2007, on my second visit to the Holy Land, I attended the Sulha.

Sulha is an Arabic word that refers to a traditional Islamic form of third-party mediation in disputes and conflicts in order to make amends. Traditionally, clans that are involved in a dispute will sit down opposite one another with a mediator and arrive at some kind of mutually acceptable settlement/compromise.

The three-letter root of sulha is s.l.h, which is the same root for the Hebrew word that means "to forgive."

The Sulha was held at the Trappiste Monastery of Latrun just outside the city of Jerusalem. My friend, a Palestinian Arab, Ibrahim Abu El Howa, was on the organising committee along with his inter-faith friends and co-workers: a Jew, a Druse, a Christian Arab, a Muslim woman, a Rabbi, a Sufi Master, a Greek Orthodox priest, an Emissary of Divine Light.

For three days, hundreds of Jews, Muslims and Christians from all countries but mainly from Israel and Palestine came together to share their experiences, their fears and hopes in an atmosphere of peaceful dialogue. No weapons were allowed on the site. Physical violence of any kind was forbidden.

By day, we sat in circles on large plastic mats in the shade of the trees and listened to the one with the talking stick. I heard an ex-Israeli soldier share that, from his mother's breast, he had been raised to hate the Palestinians and to fight for the state of Israel.

Another said that the only contact he had had with Palestinians was through the "lens" of his rifle. A Palestinian shared about witnessing his family being shot on the street in front of him for no reason. At the end of each dialogue session, there were hugs and tears, the signs of peace and reconciliation. In the evenings we engaged in sacred community rituals, singing and dancing.

The most moving experience for me was the closing ritual. The 30 or so international participants, (including me), who represented all three major Abrahamic religions, were asked to stand in a group in the central area of the site and hold the space. The Jews were asked to encircle us but to face outwards and stand still. The Palestinians were asked to encircle the Jews but to face inwards and to move clockwise looking into the eyes of every Jewish person they encountered.

Sacred music was played. The Palestinians wouldn't move. Fear and anger locked them to the land. After some gentle but persistent encouragement from the facilitator, they reluctantly took a tentative couple of steps to the left. It didn't take long before the tears started to flow. The Jews and Muslims could not continue to look into each other's eyes, witness the same soul of humanity and continue to hate. Very quickly, like a broken dam, Palestinians and Jews were crossing the great divide to hug one another. This was one of the most privileged experiences in my entire life – a rare glimpse of heaven on earth in the Holy Land.

Sense of separation (sin):
righteousness, religious superiority, selfish control of resources, limited resources, concept of enemy, concept of Infidel, murder, war

Spiritual Principles:
Oneness, Equality, Peace, Brotherhood, Sisterhood, Acceptance, Understanding, Compassion, Forgiveness, Abundant Supply, All-Sufficiency, Holy Purpose, Kingdom of Heaven is Here and Now, Love

Prayer

There is One Power – Omnipotent, Omniscient, Omnipresent Spirit. It lives and moves and has Its being within every single cell of Its Beloved Creation. It breathes Its Holy Life through and as me and through every being on the planet. Its Sacred Purpose for every beloved emanation of Itself is to reveal its Holy Face, to manifest the Kingdom of Heaven on earth in new and unique ways which have never been witnessed before and will never be witnessed again.

Every single soul who is alive on the planet now is a perfect hologram of the one Whole Life. Without him or her, this Creation would be incomplete. Each of us is divinely connected to the Holy Source of Life and thereby divinely connected to one another in an unbreakable bond of Divine Love, intrinsically joined in this Whole Expression of Divine Purpose.

I speak this Word now, declaring that the scales are falling away and Divine Purpose, Divine Calling is being heard and manifested throughout Creation. The old goals of the little separate human life are now being rendered insignificant and futile. The grand possibilities of a life lived in and for the One are now being announced in the depth of my heart and the heart of humanity since we are one and the same.

I declare that a most magnificent "YES" is being uttered throughout Creation, a conscious willingness to participate in the Divine Plan to give everything so that others may live.

I cast out of consciousness any old notions of ownership of the sacred portals of the earth. The true sacred portal is here and now. Each soul is a portal to the Divine, an instrument where the holy life of Spirit is being raised up in full awareness because the scales of humanhood have fallen away.

Down, Dirty and Divine

Furthermore, I also cast out of consciousness all false notions of Infidel or Saracen or Heathen or Pagan or Unchurched or Sinner or Blasphemer. All of God's creation is formed of Pure Spirit and this essence is eternal, pure and incorruptible.

I speak this Word of blessing upon all those who have ever seemingly murdered or been murdered in the name of God. I declare that they are now released from the karmic debt of fear and ignorance. They were simply operating out of false assumptions. The beliefs in "enemy" and "death" are now ousted. There is no power to uphold these ignorant beliefs. I cast out of consciousness all false concepts such as malecide or martyrdom - for God is a God of Life. It has never been killed. It has never killed. It has no enemies. It would never inflict suffering upon Its Own nor could It ever be the victim of suffering. It can never be divided against Itself or at war with Itself. It is Whole and includes all beings within its Infinite Self regardless of any human appearances of religion, race or creed.

I give thanks for Holy Purpose being revealed now within me and within all Creation. I give thanks for Divine Life calling all emanations of Itself into full awakening of their noble essence and of the interior crusade in consciousness to the Holy Land of the Heart. I give thanks for the release of any appearances of pain or death caused by the false notion of a religious war. I give thanks that Love prevails in the face of all appearances of evil and is, even now, as a laser-beam of Light, healing the dark dreams of the centuries. I give thanks that the New Jerusalem is established, on earth as it is in Heaven, now and forever.

I release this Word now. I name It done. And so It is. Amen.

Notes

Back to
STATION 6
Alight here for
ST. PAUL'S CATHEDRAL

St. Paul's Station is on the Central Line.
Address of Site: St. Paul's Churchyard, London, EC4M 8AD.
www.stpauls.co.uk.   Tel: 020 7246 8350.
Directions to Site: Follow signs to Cathedral from St. Paul's Tube Station.

Fig: 54:   St. Paul's Cathedral from the south west in 1896.

> "But I say unto you, Love your enemies, bless them that curse you, do good to them that hate you, and pray for them which despitefully use you, and persecute you."
>
> Matthew 5:44

> "..love as the cosmos loves: One loving itself as an other, yet remembering itself as One."
>
> David Deida

History

I deliberately left the chapter on St. Paul's Cathedral until the end because it is the culmination of everything that has gone before.

Ludgate Hill, the highest point in the City, has been a place of worship for well over two thousand years. The first Christian Church was constructed here in 604. In 1087 the Normans began the building of a huge cathedral, one of the most impressive in Europe. The grand Gothic cathedral was gutted in the Great Fire of London in 1666.

Christopher Wren had been involved in the restoration work of St. Paul's prior to the Fire but the complete destruction of the building opened up the space for something new – the recreation of the ancient Jewish Temple of Solomon in Jerusalem to prepare for the Second Coming. So instead of building another Gothic cathedral, Wren broke with tradition and designed a building in the classical Augustan style of ancient Rome – hence its similarity to St. Peter's Basilica. The distinctive dome is also reminiscent of the Dome of the Rock on Temple Mount in Jerusalem.

Fig. 55: Gothic Cathedral of St. Paul's pre-1666

As a high initiate in Freemasonry, Wren's architecture was undergirded with sacred geometry. In "The Secret History of the World," Black writes: *"The architecture of Freemasonry grows out of an occult, magical tradition of invoking disembodied spirits that goes back to ancient Egypt. 'When the materials are all prepared and ready,' it is said 'the architect shall appear'."*

The Golden Ratio (also known as the golden section, golden mean, golden number, divine proportion, divine section and golden proportion), was used by Wren extensively. The symbol for the golden ratio is the Greek letter phi Φ. This harmonious proportion is an irrational mathematical constant, approximately 1.6180339887." Scott Olsen describes it, as follows, in his book "The Golden Section":

"Phi… is one of the most elegant ratios in the universe. Defined as a line segment divided into two unequal parts such that the ratio of the shorter portion to the longer portion is the same as the longer portion to the whole, it pops up throughout nature – in water, DNA, the proportions of fish and butterflies, and the number of teeth we possess - as well as in art and architecture, music, philosophy, science and mathematics."

The symmetry, angles and proportions of this magnificent edifice are deliberately designed to usher in an atmosphere of harmony and spiritual upliftment such that a person worshipping there will naturally feel closer to God, just by being in the building, regardless of songs or sermons. The spiritual perfection of the building in form was designed to be the very portal through which Jesus the Christ would return to earth.

Relationship of St. Paul's to Temple Church

The position of St. Paul's in relationship to Temple Church is significant in the establishing of the New Jerusalem in London. When he rebuilt St. Paul's after the Great Fire of 1666, Sir Christopher Wren changed the axis of the great cathedral so that, instead of running east to west, it ran roughly 8 degrees north of east and to the same south of west. This puts St. Paul's directly in line with the Temple Church and thus Wren was attempting to mirror the relationship of the holy sites in Jerusalem – St. Paul's being a recreation of Solomon's temple and the Temple Church being the smaller representation of the Church of the Holy Sepulchre.

The Crypt

Christopher Wren was the first person to be interred in the crypt of St. Paul's in 1723. On the wall above his tomb, it says in Latin: "*Lector, si monumentum requiris, circumspice.*" ("*Reader, if you seek his monument, look around you.*")

The crypt today is largely a memorial chamber for soldiers, including Lord Nelson and Lord Wellington, who have the most magnificent tombs there. Despite the extreme male/military focus in the crypt, there are a few glimpses of the Feminine Spirit...

For example, what is fascinating is the floor of the crypt chapel. It is a mosaic made by the women of Woking Prison who were brought to St. Paul's to do the job as part of their enforced labour. They started off unskillfully but became artists by the time the floor was finished. Nice work!

Fig. 56: The floor of the St. Paul's Crypt Memorial Chapel

Down, Dirty and Divine

Florence Nightingale

Fig. 57: Memorial plaque of Florence Nightingale in crypt of St. Paul's Cathedral

The famous nurse, Florence Nightingale, is one of the few women memorialised in the crypt. In 1837 she had her call from God to become a nurse and, in 1854, despite expectations that she should become a wife and mother, she arrived in Scutari (present day Turkey) to tend to the wounded soldiers in the Crimean War. Florence Nightingale became known as the "Lady with the Lamp" because of her habit of making her rounds in the wards at night. Public funding for her mission allowed her to found St. Thomas Hospital – the first secular hospital in London.

Maria Hackett
Known as "The Choristers Friend," Maria Hackett is also memorialised in the crypt. In the early part of the 19th century, Maria was a champion for the choir boys of St. Paul's and visited cathedrals and churches all over England, making recommendations for the care and education of the choir boys. As

an unmarried woman, she travelled alone on these missions, which was both dangerous and unheard of. Maria Hackett died in 1876 and funds for her memorial plaque were donated by choristers from all over England.

Other women buried in the crypt include Sir Christopher Wren's daughter, Maria Musard Wren, from his second marriage, his granddaughter Jane and another female relative, Constantia, who was buried in 1851. The ashes of Mrs. Holman Hunt are buried there at the foot of her husband's tomb. She was the second wife of William Holman Hunt, who was the artist of the famous painting, "The Light of the World."

Princess Diana
The last person I want to mention in connection with St. Paul's, although she is not buried or memorialized there, is Lady Diana Spencer who married Prince Charles here in 1981. She was the peoples' princess, the human face of the royal family; beautiful and feminine, caring and compassionate. She died with her lover, Dodi El Fayed, in a car crash, perhaps accidental, perhaps set up, in Paris on 31 August, 1997. The nation came out to mourn her death. She opened hearts in her living and even more so in her dying.

OBE Chapel
St Faith's chapel was next door to St. Paul's. Now it forms part of the crypt and is known as the OBE (Order of the British Empire) chapel where OBE dignitaries are buried. The Order was created by King George V, in 1917, in recognition of the contribution made by women during World War I. Until then, no woman had been eligible for an award, although an exception was made for Florence Nightingale.

The Beatles were made MBEs (Member of the British Empire) in 1965. When some other MBE holders complained, John Lennon defended his band members by saying the Beatles had received their honours for entertaining people rather than killing them so they deserved theirs more. Later, Lennon returned his MBE insignia on 25 November, 1969, as part of his ongoing peace protests.

Reflection

On the architecture of St. Paul's
I was struggling with the mathematical concepts of the Golden Ratio, Pi and the Vesica Pisces. I knew all this was important to the construction of the Monument and St. Paul's Cathedral, indeed anything Wren built in London. I had been putting off writing this chapter because I knew I had to grasp these concepts and I was scared; scared that I would not be adequate to the task and that I would miss the point of the entire book and the reason I was guided to write it.

I looked up the terms on a number of websites. I tried to understand Golden Ratio for Kids, Golden Ratio for Dummies. It wasn't going in. Then I found a website with a lot of geometric shapes and patterns. I started looking at them, contemplating them. I suddenly saw three dimensions in a circle with some geometrical shapes inside it. I felt as if I were looking up into the dome of St. Paul's.

Then I stood up to make some tea. My perception of reality shifted for a split second. Suddenly I caught a vision of the universe as a swirling mass of energy, flowing harmoniously or chaotically or hardly flowing at all based on the shapes and angles the energy was held inside of.

With my intuition, I saw my apartment with new eyes. Yes, it was untidy – books, papers and files everywhere because of this writing process – but I began to see deeper, below the surface. I knew instinctively which lines and angles in my kitchen units, furniture and picture frames were "golden" and which were not. Most were not. But, miraculously, underneath all those not quite golden lines and angles and shapes, the possibility of "golden" existed. I knew that the dimension behind my outer decor was golden, perfect, harmonious, unalterable.

A conversation with Sir Christopher Wren

Then I came back to my writing table and decided to go to the source. I would ask Christopher Wren what I needed to understand. Here is what I heard as I moved within to listen:

Fig. 58:   Sir Christopher Wren (Painting by Sir Godfrey Kneller in 1711)

CW: You have to first love a straight line, then a right angle where one straight line crosses another, then a square, then a circle in the middle of the square, touching the sides of the square in four places, exactly in the middle of each side of the square. You have to appreciate the way that straight lines and curves intersect and create an infinite number of shapes and patterns. You have to see the divine imprint in the harmony and symmetry of Its creation. Sacred geometry means heavenly lines and angles. It means capturing heaven and bringing it to earth, making it not only tangible but something to dwell inside of and contemplate until all the subtle bodies of the human being are realigned in harmony. The sacred sounds of the choir in St. Paul's lifts the congregation upwards, as do the sermons with their lofty ideas. That all helps, but it is the building itself that does the work. What if the people of London could live in a city that was completely designed and constructed along the lines of sacred geometry? They would be happy, harmonious, full of praises to the Divine. Theirs would be the celestial city.

SC: I always understood that the celestial city was a state of consciousness.

CW: Yes, it is that too. Jacob's ladder goes both ways. Bringing heaven to earth. And bringing earth to heaven.

SC: What else, Christopher? What about the Tree of Life, the Jewish Cabala?

CW: Yes, this mystical Jewish diagram of the nature of the spheres and their relationship to one another was also part of my plan. It did not materialise though.

SC: Why?

CW: To create the whole city of London according to that plan was beyond my scope. I was told to focus on St. Paul's.

SC: Did you feel you were being guided?

CW: Oh yes. Every step of the way. Every drawing. It was all a mystical experience, being told how to build, how to execute God's plan.

SC: Did you believe the lost tribes of Israel were going to return to London?

CW: Yes, in the sense that anyone who was meant to be a part of the unfolding of the Grand Universal Plan would come to London. No one was lost, but simply scattered all over the world and either pulled or pushed to London to find a city of free thinkers, scientists, the end of religious bigotry. No one argues about science the way they do about religion because science can be tested and proven. Science was my love, my passion. Penetrating the mysteries of the universe, engaging in conversation with free thinkers – this was my joy. I wanted everyone to know this freedom from the chains of blind faith and suffocating dogma. St. Paul's was my testimony to the power and beauty of science, my act of praise to the Master Architect who created it all.

SC: Thank you.

On Phi, God and the Tube

I felt as if I was starting to understand Phi intuitively, but could not allow myself to include information about it in this book without some understanding of it mentally. I prayed for illumination and came across an amazing website at the 11th hour before going to print. It is: www.goldennumber.net created by Gary B. Meisner in the USA.

Meisner says that the phi number reflects God's relationship with creation. The monotheistic religions, including Judaism, Islam and Christianity, all believe that God is One and created the universe from nothing.

Look at the symbol Φ and how it is put together.

It starts with O meaning nothing.

It is then split in two by the symbol for One or Unity = I

Nothing split by Unity is Φ = Phi = 1.618 = the mathematical constant found throughout creation.

Now, here is the miracle. If you turn the Φ symbol 180° you end up with the symbol of the London Underground. That is really deep!

Fig. 59:   London Underground logo at Temple Station – Phi symbol lying down.

On the Crypt

When I first visited the crypt to do my research for this book, I couldn't help noticing that only a few token women have been immortalised here in comparison to a multitude of military males. Interestingly, the women played out archetypal feminine roles: Florence Nightingale was a nurse, Maria Hackett was a maternal figure and Diana was a nanny, a cook and a kindergarten assistant then a wife and a mother and ended her life as a lover.

This obvious imbalance led me to reflect on the polarization between men and women in religion and society. The three Abrahamic religions of Judaism, Christianity and Islam, all founded in patriarchal cultures, have automatically endorsed the false concepts that God in heaven is male and, on earth, the male is god. The Feminine Principle in Heaven has been ignored and, on earth, women have either been devalued or identified with the devil; female sexuality being seen (by men) as the reason for Adam's fall from Grace.

In the good old days of the Garden of Eden, God warned Adam and Eve not to eat from the tree of knowledge of good and evil. *For God doth know that in the day ye eat thereof, then your eyes shall be opened, and ye shall be as gods, knowing good and evil.* Genesis 3:5. She knew we would get hooked into duality, the right/wrong, good/bad game – universal hypnotism. She knew we would struggle to embrace polarities, differences and opposites.

The polarization of men and women led me to thinking about polarities in general. The nature of creation is light and dark. Polarities exist. Dualistic thinking asserts that one end of the polarity is good and the other end bad whereas they both just are. And they are both an integral part of creation.

When Jesus told us to love our enemies, I believe he meant, "Love the part of yourself that you have named wrong and projected out on to another race, another political party, a competitor or a spouse. There are no enemies out there. There is only an unloved personal shadow." His disciple, Matthew, expressed this idea as follows:

"And a man's foes shall be they of his own household." Matthew 10:36.

Consider the possibility that our notion of "hell" is really just the collective shadow – our ancient and dense, perpetuated agreement about the negative polarity of existence. If this were so, then the Devil is simply the collective shadow, personified in an evil human form.

The opposite notion might, then, also be worth considering: what if "heaven" is the collective *light* shadow and God, in the traditional understanding, is simply the light shadow personified in the form of a very good, very loving dad – a bit like Santa?

Hmmmm, if these notions were to be true, then there is no god in the commonly accepted sense but, equally, there is no devil. There is no outer authority, nor is there an outer saboteur. The play of light and dark is happening now within my own consciousness and within yours. How much of our inner light and dark do we project out on to the world and how much are we now willing to own?

Consider Phi Φ

One holy being, seemingly divided into two halves, two polarities, but ultimately whole. The number that translates to "harmony," "beauty" and "golden." Or "Divine." That is you and me.

Without our old concepts of god and the devil, we now have a massive personal responsibility for our projections and creations. If you and I are everything, and there is nothing outside of ourselves, what will we choose to bring forth in all holiness? Perhaps a real choice is available to us now, not just a kneejerk reaction to good and bad, and with that real choice, there is a capacity to dwell in an holistic reality of "Both-And," "Win-Win" and "United we stand" – the Kingdom of Heaven on Earth or, in other words, the New Jerusalem.

Sense of separation (sin):

suppression of feminine, enemy, duality (good and evil, light/dark, right/wrong, good/bad, future/past, life/death)

Spiritual Principles:

Mystical Marriage, Holy Communion, Sacred Union of all the opposites, Balance, Harmony

Prayer

There is One Power and One Presence. It includes everything within Itself. It is the Masculine and Feminine Presence in ecstatic Holy Union. It is perfect Synergy, unlimited Creativity and Life Force, birthless and deathless. This Infinite Perfection is present though and as every single cell of Creation. There is no place where Wholeness is not present.

I am Whole as a perfect emanation of the Divine. So too are all beings everywhere throughout the generations. I know that we are all connected in consciousness, we are all One at the level of the invisible Reality of the Cosmos.

From this awareness of our essential Oneness, I speak this Word for humanity declaring that the Oneness, that is true about us, is now manifesting Itself in our minds, our bodies, in our relationships and in the entire body of our affairs. Oneness with the Masculine-Feminine-Divine and within our own beings and with all beings everywhere in now established for all eternity. I cast out of consciousness all faulty or limited perceptions of self and others knowing that these misperceptions are simply nothing trying to become something.

I declare that the true relationship between all daughters and sons of the Infinite Creator is a relationship of Unconditional Love. I call forth the manifestation of this Divine Love across the planet and throughout all the dimensions in the form of acceptance, kindness, communication, service and the beholding of the Divine in all beings. I am declaring that all concepts of "enemy" or "otherness" are now dissolved. They are not true and so there is no Law to sustain them. I call forth Love into active expression between all groups that have hitherto been seemingly polarised:

Women and Men.... Muslims and Jews...... Negroes and Caucasians...... Catholics and Protestants....... Slaves and Masters ....Victims and Oppressors .... Hell and Heaven .... Dark and Light.

Where there has been an appearance of hatred, I affirm that Unconditional Love is now emerging in obvious and unmistakable ways.
Where there has been an appearance of war, I affirm that Perfect Dynamic Peace is now emerging in concrete ways.
Where there has been an appearance of conflict, I affirm that Divine Resolution is now emerging in tangible ways.

I call forth the awareness of Divine Mother, Gaia and the Feminine Face of God throughout Creation. I bless Florence Nightingale,

Maria Hackett, Princess Diana and all the renowned and nameless women everywhere who have ever surrendered themselves as instruments of love and power to bless and uplift all whom their lives have touched.

I declare that balance and dynamic harmony between the Masculine and Feminine Principles of Heaven is now established within the Earth-Body of God and, therefore, in and through the body temple of every living soul. Balance, Harmony and Wholeness has INCARNATED, become flesh as me now and as everyone who is a part of the content of my consciousness. The Planet Earth is, in truth, a heavenly body and so too are all beings who move upon it, being "in it and yet not of it."

I accept that the Masculine and Feminine Principles within my being are perfectly harmonized, in intimate holy relationship. Since I am one with the Whole, I declare that the Masculine and Feminine Principles are now harmonized in all beings and in all relationships whether heterosexual, homosexual or bi-sexual or any other –sexual. I declare that the shadow side of the human personality is now embraced, integrated and loved. It therefore no longer has power to sabotage or betray, to hurt or destroy. The Mystical Marriage, the Union of the Opposites, is now established and celebrated throughout Creation. Cosmic Consciousness is anchored and all is well.

I give thanks that this word for Unity, Balance, Harmony and Peace has now been spoken for I know that Law has already gone into motion, grounding this word of Truth in our collective experience. I give thanks that the New Jerusalem is now established in London and, indeed, everywhere on earth as it is already in Heaven. I give thanks that this Word has not fallen on rock or barren soil, that it moves with a force that cannot be resisted or denied and the Idea whose time has come is now heralded throughout all the dimensions of Reality: we are gods, we dwell now in the finished Kingdom of Heaven on earth. And we always will.

And so It is. And so It ever shall be. Amen.

Notes

EPILOGUE

Leaving St. Paul's

I imagine that you might have just left St. Paul's and are re-entering the noise and the activity of this very busy area of the City. Did you notice the beautiful engraved lettering on the glass of the revolving door as you entered? Or as you left?

"THIS IS NONE OTHER THAN THE HOUSE OF GOD. THIS IS THE GATE OF HEAVEN."

We should not assume that these words are only valid upon entering St. Paul's. They have just as much import as we exit. The House of God is everywhere.

The lyrics of the song by Rev. Dr. Michael Beckwith and Rickie Byars Beckwith (from the Agape International Center of Truth, Los Angeles, California) are singing on my mind:

"I AM in the darkness
I AM in the light
See Me if you can
Everywhere I AM"

Continuing to embrace the shadow

Do you remember Debbie Ford's wise words mentioned earlier in the chapter on the Shadow? In "The Dark Side of the Light Chasers," she told us:

"It takes compassion to own a part of yourself that you've previously disowned, ignored, hated, denied, or judged in others. It takes compassion to accept being human and having every aspect of humanity within you, good and bad. Ultimately, when you open your heart to yourself, you will find you have compassion for everything and everybody."

May this acceptance and compassion abound in you for yourself and your fellow humans.

How this book came about...

Debbie Ford has always inspired me but became an indispensible wayshower as I took the leap to write this book. I would like to share with you how it all started.

On the night of September 25th 2011, I couldn't sleep. In Austria, at the start of a business trip, I was trying to rest before work the next day but on this particular night I was paranoid about making mistakes and sleep evaded me.

In my drowsy-but-wide-awake state, I received a message: I was told that I had to write a spiritual history of London using the Tube stations as my entry point. I was also told to write down this idea so that I would not forget it in the morning.

"Yeah, yeah, yeah" I thought arrogantly, "I'll remember," but upon falling asleep, I promptly forgot about it. The next day, *they* kindly reminded me. In fact, a couple of times during that week away, *they* gave me nudges.

(Reader, I write 'they' because I am not sure how to refer to the voice inside. It feels like a crowd, not one person. I experience the voice as outside me and above me, yet it is not audible so it must come from inside me. And it is very different from my own mad mutterings or my familiar inner dialogue of self-judgment. There is a certain clarity and an urgency about it. I know if I ignore it, I will regret it even though being obedient to it is going to make me uncomfortable.)

When I returned to England at the end of that week, I settled into my morning meditation routine again and on the very first morning, as I got quiet enough to listen, *they* began a fury of downloading. *They* told me that the Tube stations were the entry point into the ground below London where people had experienced traumas for hundreds of years – traumas that had not been healed. I was told that I should research the traumas and then write a prayer to heal the pain that was still crying out for attention and assistance.

They then reminded me that people from all over the world would be converging on London for the Olympic Games in July-August 2012 and that this would be a perfect occasion for tourists to visit London and participate in the healing of the City, as well as their own healing, and the healing of the world.

Although healing is ongoing and can take place anytime and anywhere, the timing of the 2012 Olympics seemed to be the perfect springboard for this book.

With this in mind, *they* strongly suggested that the book should be published before the Olympics to support the spiritual activity undergirding this grand global event and maximize the healing potential that would become available to us all.

I said "Yes". I felt privileged to be appointed with this grand mission.

A few hours after my meditation, I recalled that there had been a strong belief a few hundred years ago that London was destined to be the New Jerusalem and that Sir Christopher Wren, who was the architect for St. Paul's Cathedral, was one of the main proponents of that movement in the 17th century.

At that point a pattern began to form in my mind. The book had already been conceived.

Prior hints from Above...

During the summer of 2011, one or two months before I really heard the message about this book, *they* kept singing the song to me: *"Turn again, Whittington, Lord Mayor of London."* Curious, I researched the story of Dick Whittington and his cat and looked up the lyrics of the song trying to understand *their* communication. Briefly, the story goes like this...

Once upon a time, there was a poor boy called Dick Whittington who, eager to seek his fortune, came to London where, it was said, the streets were paved with gold. Sadly, he soon got cold and hungry and was about to give up when, suddenly, he heard the bells of St. Mary-le-Bow chime out the rhyme, *"Turn again Whittington, thrice Mayor of London."* Dick decided to stay

Fig. 60: *The Whittington Stone. Pub sign in Archway close to the milestone where Dick is meant to have heard Bow Bells calling him back to London.*

in London and befriended a cat who was a "class-A" rat catcher. The cat helped our hero, Dick, become wealthy by catching rats for a handsome fee in the homes of London's high society.

Having made his fortune, Dick married Alice Fitzwarren, daughter of an alderman. He later became an alderman himself before being appointed as Mayor of the City of London three times in 1397, 1406 and 1419.

Fig. 61: *The milestone in Archway. (The cat was added in 1964.)*

Down, Dirty and Divine

Fig. 62:   Mural of Dick Whittington in the street entrance to the Museum of London

In actual fact, Richard Whittington was born into a wealthy aristocratic family and moved to London to trade in expensive textiles. He did not have a cat but he did marry Alice Fitzwarren and was, indeed, "thrice Mayor of London."

I reflected on the fact and the fiction and I could not figure out what *they* were trying to tell me. Things only began falling into place when I was guided to begin my research at the Museum of London a week after I had had the dream/message about writing this book. I entered the Barbican maze, where the museum is housed, from the main entrance at street level (address is 150 London Wall) and when I came through the door, there in front of me, painted on the wall, was an image of Dick Whittington!

And instead of signposts or arrows up to the museum, there was a silhouette of his cat showing the way at every turn of the stairs up to the main entrance!

When I saw the images of Dick and his cat, I knew *they* were giving me signs that I was on the right track.

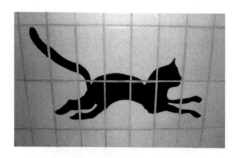

Fig. 63: Mural of Dick Whittington's cat showing the way to the Museum of London.

In retrospect, it seems like my entire life experience and spiritual journey were leading me towards becoming the scribe for this book. However, based on my old habit of resisting my roots, I would never have consciously chosen to write a book about London. Honestly, during my rebellious youth (which lasted for most of my 53 years and may not be over yet!), I really didn't have a clue about all these prods to the Prodigal on the path of homecoming.

Rebel without a clue and homeless pirate

"I didn't come here of my own accord, and I can't leave that way. Whoever brought me here will have to take me home."

Rumi

Back in the 1940s and '50s, there was a catchy British song with the refrain… "Maybe it's because I'm a Londoner that I love London town." It became a type of anthem in post-war Britain. Sadly, though, I never really loved London … that is, until I started this project.

Born to British parents in 1958 in the old Westminster Hospital, Horseferry Road — just steps away from Westminster Abbey and the Houses of Parliament — I resisted being a Brit from the start.

My parents were Londoners through and through. From my father, I received the old, common surname Clarke, which comes from the word "cleric," meaning monk. Since monks were the only literate people in medieval times, they became clerks to the nobles. Hence the nickname "Nobby Clarke," derived from "noble's cleric." My father worked for the Greater London Council. It is, perhaps, ironic that, as an adult, I would pursue a "monk-like" (yet not entirely celibate) career as a minister, teacher and scribe!

Dad used to speak to me in Cockney rhyming slang. This is the language of inner London that criminals used to confuse the police, which then infiltrated into the culture generally. So at night-time, when I was five and it was time for bed, Dad would tell me to "wash your boat-race" (face) and "go up the apples and pears (stairs) to Uncle Ned" (bed).

My mother's maiden name was Tanner. This, too, is a medieval English name originally assigned to those craftsmen who tanned hides. With her deep sensitivity towards accents as a barometer of social class in Britain, my mother would eventually enrol me for elocution lessons to counteract the Cockney accent I'd picked up as a child.

I grew up with the rags-to-riches fairy story of Dick Whittington, the sinister nursery rhyme, "Ring a ring a roses," (about mass deaths from the plague) and the macabre game, "'Oranges and lemons' say the bells of St. Clements" (about the mass executions of the Newgate prisoners). In my childish ignorance and innocence, I had no idea what all that meant.

Later, during my final years at grammar school, I experienced a significant shift in my relationship to our collective past when I studied Medieval History with a gifted teacher, Mrs. Anderson. She required we all do a "History off the Timetable" project, meaning we had to visit medieval churches, cathedrals, crypts, castles and exhibitions, and write about our impressions.

Mrs. Anderson specifically told us she did not want to read our re-writes of the guidebooks. She wanted to know how we felt, what moved us, surprised us, inspired us and repelled us. At 17, I took the train to London and dutifully visited Westminster Abbey, St. Bartholomew's Priory and the Temple Church, among other sacred sites, and still remember the awe I felt. For me, these buildings were a standing ovation in stone for the faith that the medieval builders had in God.

Today, I'm grateful Mrs. Anderson sparked within me a love of history in the form of ancient buildings I can touch and experience, illuminated manuscripts and medieval art; all this deeply enriched my travels around the world and was, perhaps, an early preparation for writing this book.

In terms of my spiritual training, I began opening up psychically in my early twenties and sat in circle as a medium after I immigrated to South Africa in my late twenties. I then spent ten years in the USA studying to be a Religious Science Minister, predominantly under Rev. Michael Beckwith at the Agape International Center of Truth in Los Angeles. (Rev. Michael is famous for his role in the well-known book and film, *"The Secret."*)

I graduated from the Agape ministerial school in 1998, and, in 1999, returned to South Africa where I established a multi-racial ministry, dedicated to the healing of Apartheid. Not only was it a successful endeavour, I loved it! However, in 2005, I felt completely burned out and came back to Britain after more than a 20-year absence from my "homeland."

Although I've lived in England now for seven years, my work regularly takes me to Central Europe and so I rarely touch down on English soil. As a "recovering reverend," I now operate in fairly thick disguise as a TEFL teacher/travelling saleswoman, promoting an English language programme in European schools.

Despite the fact that I am from London and currently represent my country and my language in my work, for most of my adult life I have been in denial of my English roots, as evidenced by my choosing to live abroad for 25 years in countries such as America, South Africa, Holland, Germany, Switzerland,

Russia and Japan. Yes, I have always been grateful to show my British passport, because it has helped me move around the world easily, and yes, I have always been grateful to be a native-speaker of English because it has helped me to study and earn a living outside the UK. But I have not been proud to say I come from London - until now.

In the process of writing, this book has become my amends to my parents, to the city of my birth and to the country of which London is the capital. It is also my amends to myself and to the shadow that I have not loved.

"Of what use to us is the wisdom of the Upanishads or the insight of Chinese yoga, if we desert the foundations of our own culture as though they were errors outlived and, like homeless pirates, settle with thievish intent on foreign shores?"

C.G. Jung

Closing words...
Thank you for coming with me on this epic journey. My prayer for you is that you receive clear signs from Spirit on your journey of spiritual home-coming. I trust those signs are even now leading you to

Heaven

on

Earth

"We shall not cease from exploration, and the end of all our exploring will be to arrive where we started and know the place for the first time."

T. S. Eliot

Acknowledgements

Mum, who listened to my dream and believed in it and in me, and who sold more advance copies of this book than anyone else in my global network.

Wendy Taylor ALSP, my kind and brilliant editor, who gave of herself unstintingly to make sure the copy and the message were one with my original voice. Wendy is a licensed spiritual practitioner at the Agape International Center of Truth in Culver City, California. She is also a copywriter, copyeditor (specializing in books, fiction and nonfiction) and a PR professional via her business, Taylor & Scott; she can be reached at wendy@taylorandscott.com

Savanna Riker RScP, who held my hand on skype through the early stages of the writing process while settling into her new home in Cairo, Egypt, amidst political turbulence. Savanna is a Religious Science Practitioner at Mile-Hi Center for Spiritual Living in Denver, Colorado and a ministerial student at the Holmes Institute. She is also a freelancer digital/virtual assistant and can be reached at www.savisgracenotes.blogspot.com or savinoelle@gmail.com

Rev. Harriet Hawkins, who prayed for me and with me throughout the writing and publishing process, thereby authoring miracles. Rev. Harriet is the Senior Minister at Unity of Tri-Valley Church, Dublin, California and can be reached at www.integralfreedom.us/blog

Andre Van Zyl and Debrah, his partner in art and life, who designed the outrageously beautiful cover. Andre van Zijl is an award-winning artist and has work in over 30 museums as well as private and public collections worldwide. Andre is also a mystic philosopher, workshop presenter on non-duality, creativity and spiritual practise. He is the published author of "Emptied of Myself," a book on meditation on the infinite self, with sacred poetry and his original drawings. Andre can be reached at www.artandrevanzijl.com

Adrian Gilbert, who encouraged me to listen to my dreams and generously wrote an endorsement for the back cover. Adrian is an author, a philosopher and a lover of the ancient mysteries. He is currently writing his 12th book and can be reached at www.facebook.com/AGGilbert1

Chris Tyler, who can capture the divine in a photograph and who painstakingly brushed all the photos and increased the resolution of all the other images in this book and on the cover. Chris does freelance portrait and commercial photography and specializes in graphic enhancement. Based in Kent, he can be reached at www.smiletakeone.co.uk

Terry Kemp, who took my headshot photo. Terry is a freelance photographer in Kent and can be reached at tj.kemp@hotmail.co.uk

J. Holmes, my dear colleague, who travelled through King's Cross Underground Station in 1987 just before the fire broke out, who got me the books I needed for my research and delivered them to my desk.

Rev. Gladys Harrison, who taught me how to pray at the First Church of United Religious Science in Johannesburg, South Africa, in 1986.

So many friends – **Lorene Belisama, Pat Norris, Jacqui Miller, Jamie Moon, Diana Arthur, Diane Hogan, Annie Cap, Becky Symmonds, Lynne Klippel, Linda Hill, Katja Edenharter** and others who have freely shared their knowledge of the publishing industry and / or prayed with me through every publishing deadline and encouraged me with various fine phrases such as: "I can't wait to get my own copy" and "I wanna read it!"

Finally, I would like to thank the **Lords and Masters of the Akashic Records** for their point of view.

Bibliography

ACKROYD, Peter: "London Under" (Chatto and Windus London. 2011)

ALEXANDER, Marc: "Haunted Churches & Abbeys of Britain" (Arthur Barker Ltd., London. 1978)

ARNOLD, Catharine: "City of Sin: London and Its Vices" (Simon and Schuster, London, 2010)

DEVIZES, Richard: "The Chronicle of Richard Devizes of the Time of King Richard the First" (Corpus Christi College Library (Cambridge), MS. no.339; British Library Cott.Ms.Domit.A.XIII. Date: 1190's) Original language: Latin. English translation by J.T. Appleby, ed. "The Chronicle of Richard of Devizes of the Time of King Richard the First." (Thomas Nelson, London. 1963) p. 65-67.

BARTLEY, Paula: "Emmeline Pankhurst" (Routledge, London. 2002.) p. 100

LAMSA, George: Translation of Holy Bible from the Ancient Eastern Text. Harper and Row, San Francisco. Originally published by A.J. Holman Co., 1933

BLACK, Jonathan: "The Secret History of the World" (Quercus, London. 2007) p. 472 & p. 476

BRANDON, David & BROOKE, Alan: "Haunted London Underground" (The History Press, Stroud, Gloucestershire. 2008)

BRUNTON PERERA, Silvia: "Descent to the Goddess: a Way of Initiation for Women" (Inner City Books, Toronto, Canada. 1981) p.8

BURKE, Jason: "Dig uncovers Boudicca's brutal streak"(Article in The Observer, Sunday 3 December, 2000.)

DEIDA, David: "Finding God through Sex" (Sounds True Inc, Boulder CO 80306. 2005)

FISCHER, Louis: "The Life of Mahatma Gandhi" (Harper Collins, London. 1997)

FORD, Debbie: "The Dark Side of the Light Chasers" (Riverhead Books, New York. 1998) p. 6 & p. 76

FORDHAM, Michael, "Jungian Psychotherapy: a study in analytical psychology" (Avon, USA. 1978) p. 5

FOX, Matthew: "The Coming of the Cosmic Christ" (Harper & Row, San Francisco, 1988)

GILBERT, Adrian: "The New Jerusalem" (Bantam Press, 2002. Corgi Books, London, 2003) p. 327

GLINERT, Ed: "The London Compendium" (Allen Lane, 2003. Penguin Books, London 2004)

GOLDSMITH, Joel: "Man was not Born to Cry" (L.N. Fowler & Co., London. 1964) p. 163

HARRIES, Richard "After the evil: Christianity and Judaism in the shadow of the Holocaust " (Oxford University Press. 2003) p. 16

HODGE, Susie: "Knights Templar" (Hermes House, London. 2007)

HOLMES, Ernest: "Science of Mind Textbook" (G.P. Putnam's Sons, New York. 1938) p. 94

IMPEY, Edward & PARNELL Geoffrey: "The Tower of London – official illustrated History" (Merrell Publishers in association with Historic Royal Palaces, 2000)

JOCHUM, Herbert: "Ecclesia und Synagoga" (Ottweiler Druckerei und Verlag GmbH, Germany. 1993)

JOHNSTONE, Michael: "The Freemasons" (Arcturus Publishing Ltd., London. 2005)

JUNG, Carl Gustav. "Psychology and Religion" (CW 11: Psychology and Religion: West and East. 1938). p.131

JUNG, Carl Gustav: "The Secret of the Golden Flower" (Harcourt Brace Jovanovich, New York. 1962) p. 144.

JUNG, Carl Gustav: "Memories, Dreams, Reflections" (Translated by Richard and Clara Winston. Random House, Canada. 1963)

KÜNG, Hans "On Being a Christian" (Doubleday, Garden City, NY. 1976), p. 169.

MARTIN, Sean: "The Knights Templar: The History and Myths of the Legendary Military Order" (Basic Books, New York. 2004) p. 35

MICHELL, John: "City of Revelation" (Abacus, London. 1973)

MOOREY Teresa: "Paganism. A Beginner's Guide" (Hodder and Stoughton, London. 1996) p. 88

OLSEN, Scott: "The Golden Section." Walker Publishing Company Inc. New York. 2006

QUINN, Tom: "London's Strangest Tales" (Portico, London, 2008)

ROBERTS, Marcus: ' Jews and the Tower of London – a Hidden History' National Anglo Jewish Heritage Trail. Fact Sheet, 2010)

ROSENBERG, Marshall B.: "Nonviolent Communication: A Language of Life" (Puddledancer Press, 2003)

SMITH, Stephen: "Underground London" (Abacus, London. 2005)

STONE, Jon R: "Expecting Armageddon: Essential Readings in Failed Prophecy" (Routledge, London. 2000)

TOLLE, Eckhard: "The Power of Now" (New World Library, USA. 1999)

WILLIAMSON, Marianne: "The Gift of Change: Spiritual Guidance for a Radically New Life" (Harper Collins, New York. 2004)

WOLMAR, Christian: " The Subterranean Railway" (Atlantic, London. 2004)

WEBSITES

www.Roman-Britain.org

www.Portcities.org.uk

www.penn.museum/

www.great-britain.co.uk

www.mathsisfun.com

www.evolutionoftruth.com

www.goldennumber.net Gary B. Meisner, copyright 2006-2011

www.newadvent.org (Catholic Encyclopedia online)

www.universetoday.com

www.cmje.org (Center for Muslim-Jewish Engagement, University of S. California)

MUSIC LYRICS

MAYFIELD, Curtis: "People Get Ready", (Album "People Get Ready," recorded by The Impressions. Label:ABC-Paramount. 1964)

BECKWITH, Michael Rev. & BYARS-BECKWITH, Rickie: "Everywhere I am" (Album "In the Land of I AM." Label: Eternal Dance Music, Los Angeles. 2000)

List of Illustrations

1. Hell in Islam. Persian. 15th century. Public Domain.
2. Yin Yang Symbol. Author: Klem. Public Domain.
3. The Rock, Mt Moriah. This photograph is from the G. Eric and Edith Matson Photograph Collection at the Library of Congress. According to the library, photographs in this collection are in the Pubic Domain.
4. Diagram of Temple of Solomon. Author: Sir Isaac Newton. Originally published within The Chronology of Ancient Kingdoms Amended by Sir Isaac Newton (1728). Source: Beinecke Rare Book and Manuscript Library, Yale University. Bibliographic Record Number 39002041693491. Image ID Number 4169349.
5. Western Wall – S. Clarke & C. Tyler
6. Dome of the Rock, Temple Mount, Jerusalem. Author: idobi, 2011. Licensed under Creative Commons Attribution-Share Alike 3.0 unported. Public Domain.
7. Dome of the Rock with Wailing Wall - S. Clarke & C. Tyler
8. Terrace of Holy Sepulchre Church – S. Clarke & C. Tyler
9. The Lamb – S. Clarke & C. Tyler
10. The New Jerusalem: Original work of art commissioned by Otto III or Heinrich II in ca 1000. Source: Bamberger Apokalypse, Folio 55 recto, Bamberg, Staatsbibliothek, MS A. II. 42. Photographic reproduction by PD-Art. Public Domain.
11. Icon of the Second coming. Greek. Ca 1700. Source: http://ikona.orthodoxy.ru/icon.php?source=source36/53 Public Domain.
12. Mind the Gap. Photo by C. Tyler. Printed courtesy of Transport for London.
13. London Bridge. Drawing from a 1682 London Map. Surveyed by: Morgan, William, d. 1690. Published: London, London Topographical Society, 1904. Public Domain.
14. Tower Bridge – S. Clarke & C. Tyler
15. Thames with Big Ben – Photo by C. Tyler
16. Cross Bones Plaque – S. Clarke & C. Tyler

17. Cross Bones, Statue of Mary – S. Clarke & C. Tyler. Printed courtesy of Network Rail UK.

18. Monument – S. Clarke & C. Tyler

19. Pudding Lane – Photo by C. Tyler

20. Spiral Staircase inside the Monument. Source: Monument website. www.themonument.info. Printed courtesy of the City of London Media Office.

21. Bank of England – Photo by C. Tyler

22. Bank Ticketing Hall – S. Clarke & C. Tyler. Printed courtesy of Transport for London.

23. Threadneedle St Tube entrance – Photo by C. Tyler

24. Mary Woolnoth Church – Photo by C. Tyler

25. John Newton. Portrait. Source: http://100megsfree4.com/dictionary/theology/tdicn.htm Public Domain.

26. Liverpool St Main entrance – Photo by C. Tyler

27. Liverpool St tube – Photo by C. Tyler

28. Bedlam. Painting by Hogarth 1732-1735. Source: The Yorck Project: 10.000 Meisterwerke der Malerei. DVD-ROM, 2002. ISBN 3936122202. Distributed by DIRECTMEDIA Publishing GmbH. Public Domain.

29. Printing Press 1568. Source: Meggs, Philip B. A History of Graphic Design. John Wiley & Sons, Inc. 1998. (p 64) Author: Jost Amman 1539 – 1591. Public Domain.

30. Altar in Crypt, St Bride's – S. Clarke & C. Tyler. Printed courtesy of St. Bride's Church.

31. Seats in Chapel – S. Clarke & C. Tyler. Printed courtesy of St. Bride's Church.

32. Old Bailey – Photo by C. Tyler

33. Emmeline Pankhurst. Ca 1913. Copyright by Matzene, Chicago. Source: United States Library of Congress's Prints and Photographs division under the digital ID cph.3b38130. Public Domain.

34. Newgate Plaque. Photo by C. Tyler

35. Old Newgate Prison. Public Domain.

36. Prison bars – S. Clarke & C. Tyler. Printed courtesy of Viaduct Tavern.

37. St. Sepulchre Church – S. Clarke & C. Tyler

38. Bell at St. Sepulchre – C. Tyler. Printed courtesy of St. Sepulchre Church.

39. St. Sepulchre tunnel – S. Clarke & C. Tyler. Printed courtesy of St. Sepulchre Church.

40. Tyburn plaque – S. Clarke & C. Tyler

41. Tyburn gallows. 1680. Source: http://www.nationalarchives.gov.uk/education/candp/punishment/g06/g06cs1s2.htm. Public Domain.

42. Charterhouse Square – C. Tyler

43. Plague boy – S. Clarke & C. Tyler

44. Palace of Westminster. Dec. 2007. Source: Selfmade stitch from 4 photographs. Author: Alvesgaspar. Public Domain.

45. Big Ben – S. Clarke & C. Tyler

46. Westminster Hall in the Palace of Westminster, London. Nove. 1808. Source: Ackermann's Microcosm of London(1808-11). Author: Thomas Rowlandson 1756 – 1827 and Augustus Pugin (1768-1832). Public Domain.

47. "Guy Fawkes in Ordsall Cave". Edition 1840. Source: Ainsworth, William Harrison. Guy Fawkes, or The Gunpowder Treason. 1840. Author George Cruikshank (1792-1878). Public Domain.

48. Kings Cross – photo C. Tyler. Printed courtesy of Network Rail UK.

49. Boudicca statue – S. Clarke & C. Tyler

50. Tower of London – S. Clarke & C. Tyler

51. The White Tower at the Tower of London. Author Bernard Gagnon, 2007. Public Domain.

52. Temple Church – S. Clarke & C. Tyler

53. Tomb of knight – S. Clarke & C. Tyler. Printed courtesy of Temple Church.

54. St. Paul's Cathedral from the south west in 1896. Source: Transferred from en.wikipedia. Author: Original uploader was Gillian Tipson at en.wikipedia. Permission: PD-ART . Public Domain.

55. Old St. Paul's Cathedral in London, engraving scanned from "An introduction to English church architecture from the eleventh to the sixteenth century," (Volume 2) by Francis Bond (1852-1918), London: H. Milford, 1913. Public Domain.

56. Mosaic floor – S. Clarke & C. Tyler. Printed courtesy of St. Paul's Cathedral.

57. Florence Nightingale – S. Clarke & C. Tyler. Printed courtesy of St. Paul's Cathedral.

58. Christopher Wren. Artist: Sir Godfrey Kneller (1646-1723) Date: 1711. Source and current location: National Portrait Gallery, London. Public Domain.

59. Temple Underground sign – S. Clarke & C. Tyler. Printed courtesy of Transport for London.

60. "The Whittington Stone" pub sign - S. Clarke & C. Tyler

61. Cat on milestone – S. Clarke & C. Tyler

62. Dick Whittington image from Museum of London – S. Clarke & C. Tyler. Printed courtesy of the City of London

63. Cat image from Museum of London – S. Clarke & C. Tyler. Printed courtesy of the City of London.

List of Colour Plates

Page 1

Fig. A. Hell in Islam. (See Fig. 1)

Fig. B. Icon of the Second Coming. See (Fig. 11)

Fig. D. The Lamb. (See Fig. 9)

Fig. C. The New Jerusalem. (See Fig. 10)

Fig. E. Dome of the Rock, Temple Mount, Jerusalem. (See Fig. 6)

Page 2.

Fig. F. Way Out sign. S. Clarke & C. Tyler. Courtesy of Transport for London

Fig. G. Temple Underground sign. (See Fig. 64)

Fig. H. Mind the Gap. (See Fig. 12)

Fig. I. Dick Whittington image from Museum of London. (See Fig. 62)

Fig. J., K., L,, Gargoyles in Temple Church – S. Clarke & C. Tyler. Courtesy of Temple Church.

Page 3

Fig. M. Golden urn and flame on top of The Monument – photo by C.Tyler

Fig. N. Statue of Truth and Justice on top of Old Bailey – photo by C. Tyler

Fig. O. Cross Swords decoration on entrance gate of St. Mary Woolnoth Church – S. Clarke & C. Tyler.

Fig. Q. Boudicca statue. (See Fig. 49)

Fig. P. Altar in Crypt, St Bride's. (See Fig. 30)

Fig. R. Cross Bones, Statue of Mary. (See Fig. 17)

Fig. S. St. Paul's Cathedral with smaller version of The Monument in the foreground – S. Clarke & C. Tyler

Page 4.

Fig. T. Beck's Underground Map. Printed courtesy of Transport for London.

ABOUT THE AUTHOR

Rev. Stephanie Clarke was born and raised in London, graduated from Bradford University with a degree in German and Russian then lived in various countries overseas for most of her adult life.

While visiting her mother in South Africa in 1985, Stephanie discovered the Johannesburg United Church of Religious Science and the Science of Mind teaching and decided to emigrate! There she had a vision of starting a multi-racial spiritual community as a forerunner to the healing of Apartheid.

This vision for South Africa led Stephanie to the USA in 1989 where she completed her New Thought Ministerial Training under the auspices of Dr. Rev. Michael Beckwith (of "The Secret" fame) at the Agape International Center of Truth in Los Angeles, California.

Returning to South Africa in December 1999, Stephanie led two workshops at the World Parliament of Religions in Capetown. In January 2000 she moved back to Johannesburg where she successfully founded a vibrant, multi-racial, metaphysical community known as Soul Home. Her greatest passion was teaching her students how to pray, the affirmative way, and leading groups to Egypt on spiritual tours. As well as Sunday services, weddings, memorials, baby blessings and teaching Science of Mind classes, Stephanie facilitated workshops on "Healing the Racial Divide post-Apartheid," "Inner Child," "Creating Ritual, Conversations with God" and "Feminist Spirituality." She was a guest speaker at international Science of Mind conferences in Russia, the Ukraine and Mexico. She was also interviewed on South African national radio and TV.

Passing the baton to her qualified practitioner students in 2005, Stephanie returned "home" to the UK where her new CELTA qualification afforded her the opportunity to teach English in Europe and Japan. Currently she lives in Canterbury and promotes English communication programmes in European schools.

Down, Dirty and Divine: a spiritual ride through London's underground is Rev. Stephanie's first book and was written based upon instructions she received in a dream on September 25, 2011.

Contact Rev. Steph

Staying in touch

Thank you for coming with me on this epic journey. I am longing to know what your experience has been. We are in this together and your insights and awakenings are an integral piece of this *pattern that connects'* all of us. I hope you will communicate with me on Facebook or via my website.

Rev. Stephanie Clarke, UK

Email: RevSteph@MinistryofLight.org

Website: www.MinistryofLight.org

Facebook Fanpage: http://ministryoflight.org/facebook

Twitter: twitter.com/Rev_Steph

Blog: ministryoflight.org/blog/

Youtube: www.youtube.com/TheRevSteph

Go to www.MinistryofLight.org/books to order more copies of **"Down, Dirty and Divine"** and see more pictures of the London sites/Tube stations.

Go to www.MinistryofLight.org/recordings to get your FREE recording of a prayer from Rev. Steph's CD "Uncommon Prayer."

Go to www.MinistryofLight.org/tours - to book a private tour with Rev. Steph around the London sites in **"Down Dirty and Divine"**.

Go to www.MinistryofLight.org/ceremonies to book Rev. Steph for weddings, baby blessings, memorials and other special occasions.

Coming Attractions!

The Miss-Adventures of an Irreverent Reverend:
a metaphysical ride through the Bible
by Rev. Stephanie Clarke

Publisher: Ministry of Light Expressions. ISBN 978-0-9567716-0-5.
Publication date: December, 2012
Elisabeth Gilbert ("Eat, Pray, Love") meets Bridget Jones and the Vicar of Dibley.
A very human story of miss-guided life experience on the spiritual journey, told with humour, candour and metaphysical interpretations of the Bible to illustrate some important life lessons.
Go to www.MinistryofLight.org for more information and to pre-order.

*****

AVAILABLE NOW!

Uncommon Prayer - a CD by Rev. Stephanie Clarke
Publisher: Ministry of Light Expressions. ISBN 978-0-9567716-1-2
A CD of ten affirmative prayers, spoken spontaneously for you, with classical music in the background, to inspire, motivate and uplift.
Go to www.MinistryofLight.org to download your FREE prayer and to order the CD.

Praise for *Uncommon Prayer*
"This wonderful CD, *Uncommon Prayer*, is my constant companion. It reminds me of who I truly am and of the endless possibilities in this magical Universe. Listening to it keeps me present and focused, joyful and light.
Thank you, Steph!"
Diana Arthur, Reiki Master, Johannesburg, S. Africa

"Stephanie is a very inspirational and warm speaker whose voice I miss and so I listen to her CD, *Uncommon Prayer*, whenever I feel down. ..."
Yuuki Hio - Physical Therapist, Kanagawa-ken, Japan

*****

SACRED TOURS

For more information about guided tours to the London sites in **Down, Dirty and Divine** or to other sacred sites in the UK and abroad, please go to the website: www.MinistryofLight.org/tours

"Travelling through Egypt with Stephanie as our tour leader was a magical, spiritual experience that brought the majesty of Ancient Egypt to life for me."
Penelope Gottlieb, Communication Specialist & Spiritual Practitioner, Johannesburg, South Africa

*****

SACRED CEREMONIES

Please contact me if you would like help in facilitating a sacred ceremony such as
- Weddings
- Memorials
- Baby Blessings
- House Blessings

or indeed any transition in your life journey which you would like to mark in a sacred way.
Email: RevSteph@MinistryofLight.org
Or go to the website for more information: www.MinistryofLight.org

*****

SPIRITUAL COUNSELLING

If you would like private spiritual counselling, please email me to set up an appointment at RevSteph@MinistryofLight.org

"Rev. Stephanie Clarke offered expertise that exceeded my years of therapy...profoundly specific insights and inspired prayer made all the difference in my world view, singing career, and self-esteem."
Cheryl Kain, singer, journalist, Massachusetts, USA

"The best friend anyone could have. Whether up or down, Steph is always willing to share with soup or that amazing laugh - a woman who has found the true meaning of life and I've been privileged to share a part of it."
Jacqueline Louise Miller, Senior Academic Coordinator, Canterbury, UK